Disability Deception

Lies Disability Educators Tell:

And How Parents Can Beat Them, At Their Own Game!

Published by:

JoAnn Collins Publishing

P.O. Box 89

Bradley Il. 60915

Orders: www.disabilitydeception.com

Printed in the USA

Library of Congress Control Number 2007902705

ISBN-10 097522501

ISBN-13 978-0-979-5225-0-5

Disability Deception

Lies Disability Educators Tell:
And How Parents Can Beat Them at their own
Game!

JoAnn Collins

1st edition

JoAnn Collins Publishing

Table of Contents

Disclaimer

This book is for educational and informational purposes only. If legal advice is required, then a qualified professional (possibly a special education attorney), should be consulted. The author and publisher are not liable or responsible to any person, with respect to any damage caused, directly or indirectly or allegedly caused, by the information in this book.

Every effort has been made, to make this book as accurate as possible; up to the time of the printing of this book.

Dedication

This book, is dedicated to my Lord and Savior Jesus Christ. Without him, this book would not be in existence.

Acknowledgements

Many people helped me with the information in this book; and I am thankful that they took the time and shared their stories with me.

I would first like to thank my three college friends Kate Dyer, Linda Aquilar, and Karen Pederson, who encouraged me to write this book and continued to encourage me along the way.

By sharing their stories, many parents helped me with this book. I am forever grateful, for their passion and insight into their children's disabilities and school experience.

Many educators shared their experiences with me for this book. I will honor their privacy by not printing their names. Thank you for your willingness to be honest and share with me your school experiences. Thank you also for encouraging me, in this endeavor.

A big thank you is due to the ladies at the Bradley Public Library in Bradley Illinois. They not only encouraged me, but helped me in numerous ways with this book. You are my favorite librarians!

A large thank you to a great attorney, Alan Smietanski, and his right hand lady, Donna Pangle. Thanks for all your help during the most difficult time of my life.

I would like to acknowledge all of the COPAA members who helped me by reading and commenting on my book, and encouraging me along the way. I have never met a more passionate group of advocates for children with disabilities. Thanks for the hard work you do every day!

Special thanks to everyone at Single Friends. Your Friendship means alot to me.

I would also like to thank all three of my children, Angelina, Courtney, and Shaun for putting up with me during the writing of this book. Shaun helped with computer work, and with the graphics for the front cover. Courtney also helped with computer work, and set up my website. I am blessed to have such wonderful children!

Introduction to the Author

JoAnn Collins lives in Bradley Illinois with her three adult children, Angelina, Courtney, and Shaun. Angelina is twenty six, Courtney is twenty four, and Shaun who is 21. Shaun and Angelina both have developmental disabilities. JoAnn received a Bachelor of Science degree in Nursing from Olivet Nazarene University in Bourbonnais Illinois. JoAnn, was thrown into the disability field; when Angelina and Shaun were diagnosed with developmental disabilities. JoAnn has been an educational advocate--a person who works with other parents to negotiate the special education system-- for over fifteen years, and has advocated at hundreds of individual educational plan (IEP) meetings. She worked at Options Center of Independent Living for over two years as the youth service coordinator and educational advocate. JoAnn has served on one advisory board with the Illinois State Board of Education, and two advisory boards with the Illinois Department of Human Services.

Introduction to the Book

The first law that required school districts to educate children with disabilities was passed in 1975. The law was called the Education for all Handicapped Children Act (Public Law 94-142). Children, with disabilities, were finally entitled to be educated by their local school districts. In 1990, the law was reauthorized; and changed to the Individuals with Disabilities Education Act (IDEA). In 2004, the law was again, reauthorized and is now called the Individuals with Disabilities Education Improvement Act of 2004. In this book, it will be referred, to as IDEA 2004. "Special education" is defined as "specially designed instruction, at no cost to the parents, to meet the unique needs of a child with a disability". (This definition was downloaded from the US Department of Education Website, **www.idea.ed.gov**).

In 1984, my daughter Angelina who had a disability, turned three years old and began to receive special education services, through my local school district. It was at that time, that I was told the first lie, by school personnel. The person, stated that "If Angelina was to get therapy, I had to pay for it." Being a parent, who didn't know my rights, Angelina received no therapy for several months, which caused her to lose the progress she had made in the Early Intervention System (EIS). Another parent finally told me about parental and student rights (the Education for all Handicapped Children Act), and I was able to get the school district to pay for Angelina's needed therapies. I have been lied to many times over the years, both for my own children, and when I am advocating for other people's children. Sometimes, I immediately recognized that I was being lied to, and other times, I did not. That is why I decided to write this book; to help a new generation of parents recognize when educators are lying to them-- and how parents, for the benefit of their child, can beat educators at their own game. That being said, I have had the privilege to work with some excellent educators who are always honest. Unfortunately, those educators who are not truthful, give the honest educators a bad name.

Parents need knowledge in three areas; in order to successfully advocate, for their child with a disability:

1. Parents must know the educational laws that they can use to help their child: IDEA 2004, the No Child Left Behind Act (NCLB), and their own states regulations for complying with IDEA 2004.

2. Parents must learn advocacy skills, strategies, and school personnel's tactics, which will be addressed, throughout this book.

3. Parents must also be knowledgeable about special education case law; in the areas that affect their child. Case law means special education cases that have been heard in due process, state or federal court, and have resulted in a decision. An organization called the Council of Parent Attorneys and Advocates (COPAA) has a lot of case law. Information can be found at the Website **www.copaa.com** (access requires a minimum yearly membership fee for parents, but it is absolutely worth it).

This book will begin with a chapter entitled "Why Do School District Personnel Lie?" This chapter will discuss reasons that professional educators think that they must resort to deception in their dealing with parents.

The second chapter will discuss general advocacy strategies that will help parents in their advocacy journey.

The third chapter will be a brief introduction to IDEA 2004 and the No Child Left Behind Act.

The remainder of the book will address important special education issues, lies educators tell, and advocacy strategies to empower parents. At the end of the book, I have included a poem that I wrote about Angelina, entitled "Dreams". Parents can help their child with a disability receive an appropriate education and live a productive life, if they are willing to advocate for them.

Chapter 1: Why Do School District Personnel Lie?

The first time I was lied to, occurred in 1984, when my daughter Angelina turned three years old, I was outraged! Why would an educator, tell me something that was not true? I bought into the myth, that school district personnel cared for Angelina and wanted what was "best" for her. I learned, fairly quickly, that the only person who really cared about my daughter's education was me. When in 1989, my son Shaun turned three, and also needed special education services, my journey into lies continued. Shaun had been diagnosed, with Attention Deficit Hyperactivity Disorder (ADHD), and speech delays at age two. He began receiving services at our local school district at age three, in 1989. The first lie I was told about Shaun was when he was six years old, and reevaluated by our local school district. I told them before the evaluation, that I believed my son had learning disabilities, and I wanted him tested in that area. Imagine my shock, when the school psychologist said that my son did not have learning disabilities, but had mental retardation. (I later learned that he never tested him for learning disabilities). I was so angry, and did not believe that my sons IQ, was as low as the school psychologist said it was. A subsequent independent evaluation, proved my son had a normal IQ (over 80), and had severe learning disabilities in seven areas. Over the years, I have been told many lies, for my own children and those I advocated for. I developed advocacy strategies to counter these lies and help all children, mine and other parent's children, with disabilities receive appropriate educational services.

School district personnel lie for many reasons. Parents must understand why educators lie, so that they can successfully overcome them, and fight for educational services for their children. The rest of this chapter will discuss why school personnel lie.

Reason 1. School personnel sometimes lie because they do not want to provide educational programs and related services to children with disabilities. Each school district seems to have a different reason for not wanting to provide services to children with disabilities. Some claim lack of money, some claim lack of time, some claim lack of personnel. A parent told me that she was told by school personnel, from her son's school, that "The state board of education won't let us give your son that service". The mother called me, and said "Why would the state board of education say that my son could not receive the educational services that he needs?" My answer to her was, "The state board of education does not determine your son's services, the IEP team does." She was shocked to learn that her school district personnel were lying. The mother wanted to know why school personnel would lie to her, and my answer was, "Probably, because they did not want to provide the needed services to your child." This book will give parents the skills to fight back, and get needed services for their children with disabilities.

I have had the opportunity to advocate at several due process hearings, to assist parents. A few of the hearings, were related to services that the child needed, but the school districts were refusing to provide.

Another way school district personnel lie to parents, is to deny that a child has a disability. Parents must be aware, when educators are lying about their child having a disability, because they do not want to provide special education services to their child. I advocated at one due process hearing when the school denied that the child had a disability. After an independent evaluation was done, the hearing officer ruled that the young man did indeed have a disability, and gave him more special education services than I asked for. I have since heard, that the young man is doing well, now that he is receiving an appropriate education.

Reason 2. School personnel sometimes lie to parents, because they don't want to provide *additional* educational and related services, to students with disabilities. I have experienced this quite a few times, educators saying that a child is making amazing progress, even though there is no objective proof of this (testing). When school personnel verbally tell a parent, that their child is making progress, that is subjective information; grades are another type of subjective information. But, when a teacher tests a child, and the testing shows educational improvement, or not, then that is objective information. I was told verbally by my son's teachers, that he was making great academic progress; until I asked for objective testing. The testing proved that Shaun's academics were far behind his peers, and that he had made little progress in his academics. It is my opinion that school personnel, told me he was making progress, because they did not want me to ask for more educational services for my son. This is a very common lie, and parents must ask for objective evidence (testing), to prove that their child is or is not making academic progress.

Reason 3. School personnel sometimes lie to parents when they ask for a specific service, because they do not want to set a precedent. I advocated for a single mother, who had a seventeen year old daughter, with learning disabilities; who was at a very low academic level. The mother had asked the school district to pay for her daughter to attend Sylvan (a private business that provides academic tutoring for school aged children), to help bring up her academic levels. The school district immediately said no for two reasons:

1. They did not want to pay for Sylvan.

2. They did not want to set a precedent of paying for outside educational services, because other parents might ask for the same service.

Reason 4. Educators sometimes, lie because they know that very few parents are going to stand up to them and continue to fight for their child. Parents often hear that they must "cooperate" with school district personnel, in order to get appropriate educational services for their child. "Cooperate" in my opinion, means letting school personnel do anything they want, which I refuse to do. What parents need to do, is to be firm with school personnel, and assertively work for the services that the child with disabilities needs, and is entitled to under IDEA 2004. I have coined this approach "assertive persistence."

Reason 5. School District personnel lie, because there is very little chance, that anything will happen to them, there is no accountability. Many educators lie during phone conversations, because they feel that it is the parent's word, against their own. The biggest lie that some school personnel tell on the phone, is to promise to provide the parent services, for their child, that they have no intention of providing. Years ago, I experienced this myself, when I was promised therapy for one of my children. Later at an IEP meeting, the school refused to put it in the IEP. The only conclusion that I could come to, is that the school personnel did not want to provide the service. I have also had other parents call me, and state that the same thing happened to them. I have a good advocacy strategy, for dealing with any verbal conversations or promises, by school personnel; and it is in Chapter 2

In my opinion, school personnel sometimes specifically lie at IEP meetings, because many of the school personnel will not stand up and defend the parent or child. Also, there is no one to hold school personnel accountable for not telling the truth.

Reason 6. Educators often lie, because they know that parents don't know IDEA 2004 well enough, to know if what they are hearing is lies. It is critical to know the laws that will assist you in advocating for your child. Knowing these laws can help you to gauge whether school personnel are telling the truth, or lying to you. As I stated earlier, when Angelina was three years old a representative of my school district, told me that I would have to pay for any therapy she needed. I did not know, at the time, that therapy is considered a related service. Related services must be provided and paid for, by the school district.

Reason 7. School personnel often lie to parents because they believe they (parents) are vulnerable; or going through a difficult time (Divorce, financial difficulty, personal problems etc). Several years ago, I was having a dispute with my school district, about increased educational services that my son Shaun needed. I invited a friend, who has a child with a disability, to go with me. One of the school personnel said that. "Perhaps Shaun is having a difficult time with his academics because of your divorce." My friend was as shocked, as I was. I looked at the school person and told them that my son Shaun had severe learning disabilities, and that he needed more intense educational services; he was not upset by the divorce. I then told the person to never say that again, and the person never did. After a few more meetings, I became fed up with the school personnel refusing to give Shaun the needed educational services. The next meeting I walked in with a letter requesting a due process hearing (See Appendix C Easy-To-Understand definitions). I eventually settled with the school district. This settlement provided my son, with the educational services that he needed, and was entitled to under IDEA (which was the educational law that was in effect at that time). Parents, whom the school district, consider vulnerable are often given a tougher time, than those parents that they do not consider vulnerable. Remember, it is not that the parent is vulnerable; it is that the school district personnel think that the parent is vulnerable!

Another group of parents, who are often given a difficult time, by school district personnel, are single parents—particularly single mothers. Two of the due process hearings I advocated at were for single mothers with children with disabilities. I believe that educators think, that such parents are probably so overwhelmed, that they will not fight for services. In my opinion, that's not true. As long as a parent, single or married, understands that they have the right to fight for their child, they very often do. I recently read an article, that stated that children with disabilities are more likely to live with a single mother, than in a two parent house. I believe that school personnel must start being less biased, to single parents, and more compassionate; in order for children with disabilities to receive an appropriate education.

Reason 8. School district personnel sometimes lie at due process hearings, because they believe that the hearing officer will believe them and not the parents. The school can usually provide six to ten witnesses who have the exact same story, and that story, is sometimes a lie. But parents usually don't have their own witnesses, that were at the meeting, other than themselves. That's, why it is important to have concrete evidence, which proves your case, as well as an independent evaluation. Since I have advocated at several due process hearings I have experienced this myself; as have other parents.

Reason 9. School personnel sometimes lie because they do not want to take responsibility if a child is not learning. In my experience, school personnel almost always either blame the parent or the child, if the child is having educational difficulties. The school personnel rarely, in my opinion, ever consider that a child's challenges could be the result of faulty curriculum, an untrained teacher, too many students, etc. It is up to parents to make sure that children receive all the services they need, and that educators are held accountable. Also, if a child is having educational difficulty, the possibility of an undiagnosed learning disability needs to be explored.

Reason 10. School district personnel often lie, to intimidate parents, and make (parents), think that they have more power than they do. I have had educators tell me many times over the years, certain things that are not allowed under IDEA 2004. If parents know the law, then they will understand when the school is trying to tell them things that are not truthful.

Chapter 2: Advocacy Strategies

I have developed these advocacy strategies, over fifteen years as an educational advocate. Whenever possible I will include resources for you to use.

Advocacy Strategy #1: Become familiar with IDEA 2004.

The statute may be down loaded at the website **http://idea.ed.gov** which is the U.S. Department of Education's website, specifically to distribute IDEA 2004 changes. *Wrightslaw: Special Education Law 2*nd Edition by Peter and Pam Wright is a book about the Individuals with Disabilities Education Improvement Act of 2004. The next chapter of this book does include a brief summary of IDEA 2004, but it is only a summary. The book is reasonably priced and available at **www.wrightslaw.com.** This book includes the law, and the regulations (instructions on how schools are to carry out the law). It also has the changes to IDEA, that were brought about in 2004 when the law was reauthorized. Take as much time as you need to read the book, and become familiar with the layout. Bring the book on IDEA 2004 with you to all meetings; and put it on the table in front of you. This will serve two purposes:

1. It lets the school personnel know that you are aware of your rights.
2. It allows you to look up any section that you need, during the meeting.

The National Information Center for Children and Youth with Disabilities (NICHCY), also has the Office of Special Education Program's (OSEP) reviewed materials, for the changes in IDEA 2004. Their Web Site is **www.nichcy.org.**

Reed Martin J.D. also has a lot of information on IDEA 2004 including two books entitled *Individuals with Disabilities Education Improvement Act 2004"* and *IDEA 2004 Making It work for You and Your Child.* These books, can be purchased at the Website **www.reedmartin.com.**

Advocacy Strategy # 2. Review your child's entire school record, temporary, permanent, E-mails and internal memos. If in a dispute with your school district, request a complete copy of your child's school record: temporary, permanent, E-mails, and internal memos.

School personnel, must allow parents to review their child's school records, if they ask to, within 45 days under the Family Educational Rights and Privacy Act (FERPA). Parents should make this request in writing. Most states regulations state that they must allow parents to review all school records sooner, so check your state regulations. Some schools require that parents call ahead and make an appointment. Parents need to know what is in their child's school record. Make copies of anything in your child's school record that you disagree with, or which helps your case. Parents should also copy their child's state and district wide testing results, and file them in a binder, for future use.

The school district is allowed, to charge a reasonable amount, for copying school records (Reasonable is defined as how much a copy costs in your area). For example: Where I live a one sided copy costs less than ten cents; so in my area that is reasonable. I have heard school districts try and charge parents twenty to thirty cents per page, to me that is unreasonable. Parents may be eligible for free copies. Most schools will give parents free copies if their children also receive free or reduced cost lunches. Ask your district for their **written policy** on school records at no charge.

If parents are in dispute with their school district, they should request a complete copy (temporary, permanent, E-mails, and internal memos), of their child's school record. I have been shocked over the years to see what is in some children's school records. A document that the parent did not know was in their child's school record, can hurt them at due process. If something in your child's school record is inaccurate, ask that it be blackened, out with a magic marker. IDEA 2004, allows items in a child's school record, to be removed, if the parent feels that it is not true, or inaccurate.

*Once you are familiar with IDEA 2004, and have reviewed your child's entire temporary and permanent school record (and received copies of your child's school record, if needed), you are ready for Advocacy Strategy #3.

Advocacy Strategy #3:   Begin creating concrete evidence, within your child's school record.

   The best way, to communicate with school personnel is by writing letters. The letters that you write will be your evidence in case you have a dispute with your school district, or ever end up in due process. Letters, should be typed if possible. If hand written, be sure and keep a copy. All letters written to school personnel, about your child, must be kept as part of your child's school record.

   Below is an example of a letter, sent to school personnel by a parent:

Name of school district representative
Name of school district
Address
City, State and Zip Code
                                        Date
Dear

   I am writing you this letter today about my son Tommy who is nine years old and in the fourth grade at XXX. At Tommy's IEP meeting on March 15 of this year, I stated my concern that Tommy is not making progress in learning to read. It is critical that Tommy be given testing, to determine what his reading level is, and what his educational needs are. From there we can determine what curriculum will be used, to teach him to read. IDEA 2004 and the No Child Left Behind Act require that curriculum be research based.

I am requesting that Tommy be tested using the Woodcock Reading Mastery test, by his special education teacher, within fourteen school days. The Woodcock Reading master test is a comprehensive reading test that includes decoding scores and vocabulary scores; which I believe Tommy needs. I expect to receive the parent consent form within five days of you receiving this letter. After the testing I am requesting an IEP meeting to discuss the results and to determine what "research based" reading program will be used to teach my son reading. Could you please send me a copy of the results, at the same time as the ten day written notice, so that I will be prepared to participate as an equal member of the IEP team.

Miss Smith

Address

City, State, and Zip Code

This letter documents that you told the school district of your concern, and that you are requesting testing, to determine your sons reading level. While state or federal law, does not state that parents have the right to ask for a specific test; parents should ask anyway, if there is a specific test that they feel their child needs. The Woodcock Reading Mastery Test has decoding and vocabulary, which is why I like it, and ask for it often. The letter should be as clear as possible, and should include specific timelines. Each letter sent to school personnel should contain a hand written signature. The letter must be hand delivered to the special education person's office or sent by certified mail with a return receipt, (which could be costly). Parents must keep copies of all letters sent to educators. Any letter sent to the school district, becomes part of your child's school record.

If you do not hear from the school within ten days, write them again. Below is an example of a follow-up letter, to use, if you receive no written response from the school.

Name of School District Representative

Name of School District

Address,

City, State, and Zip Code

Date

Dear

 I have received no response from my request; that Tommy's teacher conduct a Woodcock Reading Mastery test. If I do not hear from you within seven school day's I will have no choice but to file a complaint with the state board of education. I am trying to work with you so that my son Tommy can learn to read and receive a Free Appropriate Public Education (or FAPE).

Miss Smith

Address

City, State, and Zip Code

 Write letters whenever you need to, and always answer any written correspondence from the school. Don't forget, to date the letter, and sign it at the bottom. Copies of letters, must be kept. It is useful for filing letters by date in a three ring binder; older letters on the bottom, newer letters on the top. By writing letters, you will be developing concrete evidence to help you win a dispute with your school district. Also, keep copies of the letters that are sent to you, by school personnel.

 Parents should start a filing system, to keep all documents that they may need in the future, if a dispute arises with school personnel. A three ring binder, can be used for this. Parents should save teacher notes, child's school work, suspension notifications, daily behavior sheets, school personnel E mails, report cards, updates of student progress, and state and district wide testing scores.

Advocacy Strategy #4: Any important educational issue for your child, should be handled in writing, and not verbally. Verbal conversations with school personnel should be limited to minor issues.

Any spoken conversations with school personnel, should be followed up, with a letter. The letter is your documentation that the conversation actually happened, and puts in writing any promises made. Below is an example of a letter to document a conversation.

Name of School District Representative
Name of School District
Address
City, State and Zip Code

Date

Dear

I was glad that we were able to have a phone conversation about the request I made for a Woodcock Reading Mastery Test for my son Tommy. I was quite surprised when you became angry about my request; and accused me of calling Tommy's special education teacher a bad teacher. I never stated that Tommy's teacher was a bad teacher. What I stated, is my belief, that my son Tommy is not learning to read, and needs the testing. IDEA 2004 states that materials used to teach academics, should be "research based." What that means is proof that the materials work in teaching children to read. There are many studies that prove that simultaneous multi sensory reading programs such as the Orton-Gillingham methodology are effective in teaching children to read.

I will expect, to receive the parent consent form, within a few days. When the testing is complete, I would appreciate a copy of the results, before the IEP meeting, so that I will be prepared to discuss the results at the meeting.

Miss Smith

Address

City, State and Zip Code

The school person may write you back, and say it didn't happen like this. You would write them another letter, and state that you stand by your version of the conversation. Keep a copy for yourself; and put it in your 3-ring binder.

Information on the Orton Gillingham methodology is available at the Website **www.ortongillingham.com.**

I was advocating at a due process hearing, for a sixteen year old young man. His teacher stated, to his mother, that the restrictive placement the school was offering was not appropriate for the young man. When his mother told me, I was so excited. I typed a letter to the teacher, from the mother, documenting what the teacher said during the conversation. The next time the mother saw the teacher, she hand delivered a copy of the letter to the teacher; and observed the shock on the teacher's face. I eventually settled that case, to the betterment of the young man, and I credit that letter and what the teacher said to winning the case. Documenting what educators say can have huge positive impact for parents and children. I write letters to document conversations for two reasons:

a. It summarizes the content of the verbal conversation, in writing. These letters can be used, in due process or court as evidence, recollections of verbal conversations would be considered hearsay, and would not be allowed.

b. I hope that school personnel will be more careful what they say, if they know that a parent will be sending a letter, documenting the conversation.

Advocacy Strategy #5: At the IEP at the end of the school year, ask that testing be done, in all academic areas, at both the beginning and end of the next school year.

I borrowed this suggestion from Pam and Peter Wright's book *From Emotions to Advocacy*. IDEA 2004 now requires, that IEPs include present levels of academic functioning. It previously stated, that present levels of functioning needed to be written on the IEP, but the word "academic" was added. In my opinion, the only way the school can honestly put present levels of academic functioning on the IEP is to do pre and post testing. Parents need to be assertive in asking for this to be written on their child's IEP. For Example: Your seven year old daughter, with a learning disability, will begin second grade. At the IEP at the end of first grade, ask that her academics (reading, writing, spelling, and math etc) be tested at the beginning and end of second grade. That way, the school district personnel can come to the IEP at the end of second grade and honestly give present levels of academic functioning. Testing is objective proof that your child is making progress in all academic areas.

If you have concerns about your child's functional skills, ask that pre and post testing in functional areas be done also.

Advocacy Strategy #6: Be as positive as possible with school personnel, but be firm. I call this "assertive persistence."

The first advocacy tip I ever learned is to "Repeat! Repeat! Repeat!" For example: If you are in an IEP meeting, trying to get speech therapy for your child, the school may try and change the subject. Say, "I am sorry we were discussing why my son needs speech therapy." Repeat! Repeat! Repeat! Parents should be assertive, but should never be aggressive. Aggressiveness, is defined as cussing, screaming, and yelling. Assertiveness is defined, as being clear with what you are asking for, and doing it in a firm way; not resorting to aggressiveness.

Try and bring up positive issues whenever possible; especially if school personnel are doing something to help your child. When my children were in school, I was always careful to bring up good things, that school personnel were doing as well as negative things.

Advocacy Strategy #7: If you are attending an IEP meeting, and are in a dispute with your school district, consider writing a parent input statement, to bring to the meeting.

A parent input statement is a short letter that states what services, or placement your child needs etc. This is a chance for the parent to have something in their child's IEP, that expresses their opinion. Since you will bring it to the IEP meeting it does not have to look like a letter. Below is an example of a parent input statement.

Parent Input Statement   Date

By Miss Smith for Tommy Smith

I am so thankful that you decided to test my son Tommy using the Woodcock Reading Mastery Test as I had requested on Date. XXX. I also appreciate you sending me a copy of the test results before the meeting, so that I can be an active participant. My son is nine years old and in fourth grade. The Woodcock Reading Master Test showed word identification at a grade equivalent of 1.7, word attack (decoding-breaking down the word) of 2.7 and a basic skills cluster with a grade equivalent of 1.9. That means that my son who is in fourth grade is delayed by more than two years in reading skills. Since we know what level he is reading at we now need to decide together how to help him make progress. My research shows me that a simultaneous multi sensory reading programs, such as the Orton-Gillingham Methodology, has had great success in helping children learn to read. I would also like to discuss teacher training in the methodology that we determine my son needs.

Keep the input statement short (maximum of one page), and bring one copy for each person who will be attending the IEP. Make sure that the school personnel attach the parent input statement, to your child's IEP. If they refuse to attach the parent input statement to the IEP refer to Strategy #8 and consider filing a complaint with your state board of education.

Advocacy Strategy #8: If your school district violates IDEA 2004, consider filing a complaint with your state board of education.

The Office of Special Education Programs (OSEP), which is part of the Department of Education, has a Website at **www.ed.gov,** where it lists several items that need to be included in a state complaint.

1. A statement that a school district.has violated a requirement of Part B of IDEA 2004 or its regulations.

2. The facts on which the statement is based.

3. The **signature** and contact information of the complainant. (Parent signature)

4. If alleging violations regarding a specific child:

a. The name of the child and the child's address.

b. The name of the school the child is attending.

c. In the case of a homeless child; contact information for the child and the name of the school the child is attending.

d. A description of the nature of the problem of the child, including facts relating to the problem (this means what is the violation of IDEA 2004, and any facts related to the violation).

5. A proposed resolution of the problem, to the extent known and available, to the party filing the complaint, at the time the complaint, was filed.

A parent, may either file an individual complaint, for their own child, or a systemic complaint for other children with disabilities, in their district. Several year ago, I filed a systemic complaint against my school district related to copying fee for school records. Since I had a complaint, I believed that other parents in my district did also. That is why I filed a systemic complaint. I ended up winning th complaint, and the state board of education told my school district that they shu give each parent a copy of the school's policy on fees for copying school record Also, I did not have to pay for the copy of my son's school records. Below is an example of a letter to file an individual complaint.

State Board of Education

Address

City, State, and Zip Code

Date

Dear

My name is Miss Smith and I would like to file a formal complaint against (school district name and number) for violating the rights of my son, Tommy Smith, under IDEA 2004. My son Tommy is nine years old, with a Birthdate of, and is in the fourth grade at Martin Elementary School.

Tommy has been having difficulty with reading. I asked the school to give him a Woodcock Reading Mastery test, so that we could determine what level he reads at. The test, was administered by his teacher, and an IEP meeting was called. A discussion was held on what type of instruction Tommy needed to help him learn to read. I have been investigating what curriculum is "research based" as IDEA 2004 requires. I asked that we discuss the Orton-Gillingham Methodology of simultaneous multi sensory instruction. The school refused to discuss this methodology, and stated that they were going to continue using the same curriculum that they were using previously; which has not been successful in teaching him to read.

The violations that I believe they committed are:

1. Under IDEA 2004, parents are equal participants in the IEP process. By refusing to discuss the curriculum that I believe my son needs, the school district violated my rights as an equal participant, in the IEP team.

2. IDEA 2004 requires that any curriculum used be "research based" and proven that it works to help children learn. The school refused to show me, in writing, proof that the curriculum they are currently using is "research based." The school district is violating my son's rights to FAPE by continuing to use a curriculum that is not teaching him to read.

3. The school district is violating my son's rights, by not taking into account his educational needs as IDEA 2004 requires. The school is doing this, by not offering my son enough remediation for his reading difficulty. School personnel state that thirty minutes a day is all the time they can offer him for help with his reading difficulty. I do not believe that this meets my son's needs, or will help bring his reading level up to his grade level.

4. The school district is violating my son's rights, by refusing to discuss teacher training, for the reading method that we choose. If the teacher, is not properly trained, then the method will not be successful in teaching my son to read.

Proposed Resolution

1. The school district should be required to hold another IEP meeting, and openly discuss the curriculum that I believe will help my child learn to read. I believe that my son needs a simultaneous multi sensory reading program in order to learn to read, and am willing to discuss this at length with school personnel. School personnel, should also be instructed, to give reasons why they are refusing to use a simultaneous multi sensory reading program for my son, what they are offering instead, and reasons why.

2. IDEA 2004 states that curriculum must be "research based." The curriculum that I am recommending is "research based," and is used to teach many children with disabilities to learn to read. The school district wants to continue to use the same curriculum that has been ineffective in teaching my son to read.

3. The school district must offer my son, the amount of reading remediation that he requires to meet his individual needs. If my son, needs one and one half hours a day of reading remediation, instead of the one half hour a day the school district is offering to receive FAPE, the school is required under IDEA 224 to provide it. Perhaps the extra instruction could be given before or after school. School personnel should be required to show proof that the amount of reading remediation time they are offering my son, will meet his unique educational needs.

4. During the IEP meeting, the school district should be required to discuss teacher training, and be willing to include it in my child's IEP, if needed.

I am enclosing a copy of my son's IEP. Please send me, copies of all correspondence from and to the school district. I would appreciate if any contact about this complaint, be in writing. I expect to hear from you in writing, within ten days, and will expect a resolution of this complaint within sixty days, as required by IDEA 2004.

By Mary Smith

Address

City, State Zip

Attach to the complaint any evidence that you have of the violation. In Illinois, the investigation is usually limited; most of the time it includes whatever evidence the parent sends in. In the complaint, don't forget to add the resolution that you would like to see to your complaint (what you want the school to do to resolve the complaint). The state board of education has ten days in which to respond to your complaint, and sixty days to resolve it. Several violations may be put in one letter.

If the state board of education calls you on the telephone, tell them that you would prefer any communication about the complaint, be in writing. It is my experience, that sometimes, state board of education employees, try and talk a parent into withdrawing the complaint; which they should not do. This will also give you documentation about how the complaint is being handled, in case you need it in the future.

Some states have sample complaint forms on their Web site. If you are interested in using a form to file a state complaint, check your state board of education's website, to see if you can find a form. If you cannot find the form, contact your state board of educations—special education department; and ask them for a complaint form.

Advocacy Strategy #9:   If you are having a dispute with your school district, over services your child needs, consider getting an independent educational evaluation (IEE).

Independent educational evaluations, and independent educational evaluations at public expense, will be discussed in Chapter 5. IDEA 2004 states that schools must "consider" any independent evaluation the parent brings to the school. Make sure the evaluator you pick, has the appropriate credentials, and meets the school districts requirements for reimbursement. For example: a speech pathologist can do a Speech/Language independent evaluation. Make sure the evaluator is willing to write a report, with specific information in the report, about what services your child needs. Also, if the dispute is over amount of services and goals, make sure the independent evaluator includes these items in the written report. When my son was in school, I used to take him to a psychologist that specializes in children who have learning disabilities, every year for testing. She would write a report about what services he needed for the next school year. I felt that the school personnel would listen more to what my son needed, if it came from a psychologist who was familiar with children with learning disabilities, rather than me.

The best way to find a good evaluator is to ask other parents, of children with disabilities, or a local disability organization. For Example: If your child has dyslexia, check with local dyslexia organizations, and see if they can refer you to a qualified evaluator. If that is not possible, every state board of education should have a list of independent evaluators on their Web site. Reed Martin J.D. has a link to all the state board of educations on his Website **www.reedmartin.com.**

The list of evaluators from your state board of education is available if a parent needs it, but parents are not required to pick a person from the list. Parents can also contact a parent training and information center (PTIC) in Advocacy" by Peter and Pam Wright. their state. A list of the PTICs in every state is in the book *From Emotions to Advocacy* by Peter and Pam Wright.

Advocacy Strategy #10:   Consider tape recording IEP meetings.

Most districts do not like it and usually put up some type of resistance. The benefit to tape recording is that you have evidence of anything they say, the downside is that they may not say much, because they know they are being recorded. Parents should tell their school district personnel that they intend to tape record the meeting, so that they can be an equal participant in the meeting.

OSEP issued a memorandum 91-24 on July 18, 1991 that discussed their policy on tape recording of IEP meetings. "State board of educations or public agencies may have a policy against tape recording of IEP meetings, but according to this memo, it may be challenged under the US constitution." "Thus, any policy limiting or prohibiting a parent's right to tape record the proceedings at an IEP meeting must provide for **exceptions** if they are necessary to ensure that the parent is able to understand the proceedings at the IEP meeting. . . It should also be noted that under certain circumstances, an SEA or local district policy limiting a parent's right to tape record an IEP meeting could also constitute a violation of Section 504 of the Rehabilitation Act of 1973, the federal law that prohibits discrimination. . .on the basis of disability." This would of course apply if the parent had a disability.

On September 29, 1992 OSEP published its Question #12 opinion in the Federal Register specifically interpreting IDEA IEP meetings and stated "**that it is permissible to tape IEP meetings at the option of either the parents or the agency.**" Federal Register, Vol. 57, No. 183, September 29, 1992.

There have also been 2 Connecticut court cases on the issue of tape recording IEP meetings. In E.H. and H.H. v. Torozzi 16 EHLR 787 (D. Conn. 1990) the court stated that the parent's right to participate far outweighed the District teacher's asserted right not to be recorded. In V.W. and R.W. v. Favolise, 16 EHLR 1070 (D.C. Conn.1990. the court also upheld the parent's right to tape record the IEP meeting. The court reasoned that parents have a statutory right to attend and participate in IEP meetings and, the district could not legally engage in an act to limit the parents rights.

If the school district, refuses to allow tape recording of IEP meeting's, you have three options:

1. Reschedule the meeting and consider filing a complaint with your state board of education.

2. If the school district personnel state that taping IEP meetings is against district policy, ask to see the policy. If they have a district policy, preventing taping of IEP meetings, ask for a copy. After you have received a copy, ask for an exception, under OSEP's policy letter. A parent could state that they need to tape record the meeting so that they can understand the meeting and be a full member of the IEP team. Parents should also quote the Federal Register Question #12, where OSEP states that **it is permissible to tape IEP meetings at the option of either the parents or the agency.** If school personnel still do not allow you to tape record an IEP meeting, take the district policy, and file a complaint with the state board of education. Don't forget to tell them that you asked for an exception under OSEP's policy and about the Federal Register #12 question from OSEP.

Advocacy Strategy #11:   Parents must be willing to stand up to disability educators, and make them prove what they are saying is the truth or not.

My own school district personnel would on occasion tell me things that I knew were not true. I was having a dispute with my school district over unilaterally graduating my son because he had enough credits. I asked school personnel to show me in IDEA where it states that schools have that authority, and they were not able to show me. There was a court case in the state of Illinois called *Kevin T. vs. Elmhurst Community School District No 205,* which discussed unilateral graduation. The judge ruled for Kevin T's parents; that he needed education beyond the age of 18; and that the school district could not unilaterally graduate him.

IDEA 2004, states that children with disabilities must be prepared, for post school learning, jobs, and independent living. IDEA 2004 also requires that a child's functional levels be determined, and addressed. If a child has enough credits, but is at a low functional level, is not ready for independent living, has received no job training, or transition skills, they need to continue being educated at school.

School personnel, must be held accountable for their lies, and I am hopeful that as parents continue to make them accountable, they may stop saying things that are not true. I know "Keep dreaming!"

Advocacy Strategy #12: Get a copy and become familiar with your states regulations for special education.

Every state must write regulations on how they are going to comply with IDEA 2004. In the book *From Emotions to Advocacy* by Pam and Peter Wright there is a list of all of the state board of educations; where you can write for a copy. I always bring the federal rules for IDEA 2004 with me but I also bring my

Illinois Administrative Code. I find that school districts like to use the state regulations, more than the federal regulations.

The state regulations should be available on your state board of education's Web site. Go to **www.reedmartin.com** and click on state board of educations and look for your states regulations.

All states will have to rewrite their regulations to include all changes brought about by the reauthorization of IDEA in 2004. Contact your state board of education and see if the new regulations are available yet. At the writing of this book the regulations for my state, Illinois, were not yet completed.

Advocacy Strategy #13: Become familiar with the No Child Left Behind Act of 2001.

The U.S. Department of Education puts out a great free booklet on No Child Left Behind. The booklet is entitled "No Child Left Behind Parents Guide." This booklet can be ordered by calling 1-800-872-5327 or on their Website at **www.gov/pubs/edpubs.html**. It is easy to understand and explains how the law affects all children in Title 1 schools, including children with disabilities. Peter and Pam Wright also have a book entitled *No Child Left Behind* ,which can be purchased at **www.wrightslaw.com.**

Reed Martin also has a book on the No Child Left Behind Act entitled No Child With A Disability Left Behind. This book can be purchased at **www.reedmartin.com.**

I believe that the No Child Left Behind Act is going to be responsible for many children with disabilities learning to read and do other academics.

Advocacy Strategy #14: If you need more information about special education, or specific help with your child, contact a parent training information center (PTIC) and or a Center for Independent Living (CIL).

A list of the PTICs is in Appendix E of *From Emotions to Advocacy* by Pam and Peter Wright. The parent training information centers may offer staff members to attend IEP meetings with parents. PTICs also offer trainings for parents, that are affordable and parent friendly.

Many of the Center for Independent Living have a person that works with children services and educational advocacy. For a complete list go to the Website **www.virtualcil.net/cils.**

Advocacy Strategy#15: Always read the IEP before you leave the meeting.

I have had experiences where I have not read the IEP, and was surprised when I did. I found things written on the IEP that I disagreed with, and some important items were left out. When you read it, make sure that any discussions that occurred about your child, are included in the IEP. Check goals, and also check the page of services to make sure all services agreed to, are in writing, with proper minutes. Also check the wording of the services, to make sure that they are written in a way that every one understands how they are to be given, and also the right amount.

While IDEA 2004, does not state that school districts must have a parents signature, to start implementing the IEP (except for initial services); I have heard from many parents, that their school district is requiring a parent signature, before the IEP can be implemented. Parents should check their state regulations, to see if their state requires a parent's signature. If your state does not require a parent's signature on the IEP; then I would ask school personnel "By what authority are you stating that a parent must sign the IEP, before it is implemented?" If the school district states that they will not implement the IEP without your signature, and your state does not require a parents signature before the IEP is implemented, consider filing a state complaint.

Chapter 3: Brief summary of IDEA 2004 and No Child Left Behind

The Education for all Handicapped Children Act (94-142), was passed in, 1975. This act, was passed, six years before the birth of my daughter Angelina, who was diagnosed with severe mental retardation. Angelina started in the special education system in 1984, when she was three years old, In 1990 the law was changed to the Individuals with Disabilities Education Act. In 2004 IDEA was reauthorized, and became IDEA 2004. In this book, IDEA will be referred to, as IDEA 2004.

When Congress passed IDEA 2004, they wrote Findings, which explain why they felt it necessary to have an educational law for children with disabilities. These findings are located on the Department of Education's Website for IDEA 2004 changes. The Website is **http://idea.ed.gov.** Since the enactment and implementation of the Education for all Handicapped Children Act of 1975, this title has been successful in ensuring children with disabilities and the families of such children access to a Free Appropriate Public Education and in improving educational results for children with disabilities. However, the implementation of this title, has been impeded, by low expectations and an insufficient focus on applying replicable research and proven methods of teaching and learning for children with disabilities. Congress also stated that special education would be better if: "Having high expectations for such children and ensuring their access to the general education curriculum in regular classrooms to the maximum extent possible . . .(to meet developmental goals and to the maximum extent possible to meet the challenging expectations that have been established for all children. Be prepared to lead productive and independent lives to the maximum extent appropriate". Another part of IDEA 2004 that is important, for parents to understand, is the purpose. The purpose is to "Ensure that all children with disabilities have available to them a free appropriate public education that emphasizes special education and related services designed to meet their unique needs and prepare them for further education, employment, and independent living." Most school districts offer a one-size-fits-all special education program, rather than offering a program specific to the child's educational needs, as IDEA 2004 requires. Years ago, when I worked as an educational advocate for a center of independent living, I came up with a theory for this and I call it the "square peg/ round hole theory." What this means is that children with disabilities are unique, and thus could be called "square pegs." Most school districts only have "round holes", and so they are going to attempt to ram the square peg into the round hole until the corners break off; and the square peg fits into the round hole. Under IDEA 2004, school districts need to develop a special education program, that meets the unique educational needs of every child, with a disability. Special education is a service not a place. A child can receive special education services in the regular education classroom or in a self-contained classroom; whatever is appropriate for that child to learn.

There were many changes brought about in IDEA 2004; and they are located throughout this book. Below are a few:

1. Mandatory Medication is Prohibited.

In IDEA 2004 under "State Eligibility" it states that school personnel are prohibited from insisting a child to take medication, such as Ritalin or Adderal, to attend school, receive an education, or receive special education services.

2. **Specific Learning Disabilities**.

IDEA 2004 states that "The law has moved away from using a discrepancy model (difference between a child's potential and actual academic functioning level), to identify children with specific learning disabilities. School personnel are not required to determine if the child has a severe discrepancy between achievement and intellectual ability; to find that the child has a specific learning disability. The school may use response to intervention to determine if the child responds to scientific, research based interventions as part of the evaluation process." This is an important change; because I have experienced school personnel denying services to children with learning disabilities, by using the discrepancy formula, and stating that the child was working at their potential.

3. FAPE Requirements. IDEA 2004 now requires school districts to ensure that a free appropriate public education (FAPE), is available to any individual child with a disability, even though the child has not failed, or been retained in a course, and is advancing from grade to grade.

4. Mediation, Due Process and Resolution Meetings. A lot of changes have been made and will be discussed in Chapters eight and nine.

The No Child Left Behind Parent Guide (which is available free of charge on www.nclb.gov/next, states: "The No Child Left Behind Act of 2001 is designed to improve student achievement and change the culture of American Schools". The No Child Left Behind Act applies to all public schools that receive Title 1 money. Title 1 funding is from the Federal Government and "supports programs to improve the academic achievement of children of low income families". According to the *No Child Left Behind Parents Guide, NCLB:*
a. Supports learning in the early years to prevent learning difficulties in later years.
b. Provides more information for parents about their child's progress.
c. Alerts parents to important information on the performance of their child's school, by requiring school districts to print yearly report cards.
d. Improves teaching and learning by providing better information to teachers and principals.

e. Ensures that teacher quality is a high priority.

Definition on "highly qualified teacher" is a teacher that has full state certification, holds a license to teach, and meets state requirements.

f. Gives more resources to schools, in additional funding.

g. Allows more flexibility, in exchange for more accountability.

h. Focuses on what works based on scientifically based research.

No Child Left Behind requires many things, including:

a. Testing. The purpose of state assessments according to the *No Child Left Behind Parents Guide* ". . .is to provide an independent insight into each child's progress as well as each schools progress." School personnel must test 95% of students of various subgroups (those with disabilities, or who speak English as a second language etc). School districts set annual yearly progress goals (AYP), that they must meet. If they do not meet, the annual yearly progress (AYP) goals for two years, steps must be taken, which include school choice and independent supplemental educational services; tutoring.

b. Extra help with reading in the early years (kindergarten to third grade). "Reading First" grants are federal grants given out to school districts to help them in this area. Check with your district and see if they are receiving one. NCLB has defined five components of reading, so that parents can check and see if the reading curriculum their school is using contains these five components   If the curriculum does contain these five components then children will have a better chance of learning to read.

    The five components are:

1. "Phonemic awareness," or the ability to hear and identify sounds in spoken words.

2. "Phonics" or the relationship between the letters of written language and the sounds of spoken language.

3. "Fluency" or the capacity to read text accurately and quickly.

4. "Vocabulary" or the words students must know to communicate effectively.

5. "Comprehension" or the ability to understand and gain meaning from what has been read.

Parents must make sure that their child's reading curriculum, contain these five components.

c. Scientifically-based research. This requires that the educational program has been proven to work to teach children. Schools often use curriculums that are not proven to work, and this negatively affects children's abilities to learn to read. It has been my experience, in fifteen years as an advocate, that children with disabilities learn academics better if the curriculum used is multi sensory.

d. Creating safer schools. This targets violence in schools that prevent children from learning.

e. Choice of schools, supplemental educational services, and timelines. This section discusses how parents get to choose schools, how to get supplemental educational services, and the timelines the schools must meet.

I always encourage parents of young children with disabilities to learn as much as possible about No Child Left Behind. I believe that this law is going to make it possible for thousands of children with disabilities to learn to read. The only negative part of this law that I can see, is that the US Department of Education is making decisions, that appear to be watering down the law. Increased timelines, leaving some children out of testing numbers, waivers, etc. These will have a negative impact on the ability of children with disabilities to achieve academic success.

At the writing of this book, the No Child Left Behind Act, is up for reauthorization. A study by the Center on Education Policy, shows that children are doing better, on state reading and math tests, since No Child Left Behind was passed five years ago. The US Education Secretary Margaret Spellings, has made a statement, that No Child Left Behind is working and should be reauthorized.

Appendix A, of the *No Child Left Behind Parents Guide,* contains information on Topics of No Child Left Behind.

Adequate Yearly Progress: **www.nclb.gov/start/facts/yearly.html**

Accountability: **www.nclb.gov/next/faqs/accountability.html**

Charter Schools: **www.nclb.gov/start/facts/charter.html**

School Choice: **www.nclb.gov/mext/faqs/choice.html#l**

Supplemental Educational Services:

www.nclb.gov/parents/supplementalservices/index.html

What Works Clearinghouse on Education Research:

www.w-w-c.org

Chapter 4: Initial Evaluations, Reevaluations, and Eligibility for Special Education

Evaluations are one of the areas where parents frequently disagree with school personnel about. Evaluations are important for several reasons:

1. They help diagnose a child's disability.

2. They give academic levels, they give adaptive behavior scores (activities of daily living, social skills, etc).

3. They help determine what a child's educational needs are.

Parents and school personnel must understand what the child's disability is; before they can work out a plan to educate them. Many times, I have become involved with a child who did not have his or her disability identified properly; and this had a negative impact on the child's education. I will begin this chapter by discussing lies associated with evaluations, and how parents can overcome them, for the good of their child.

Lies about Initial Evaluations

1. "Our district only takes referrals for special education services from teachers, not parents."

IDEA has always allowed referrals from anyone including parents. IDEA 2004 added a specific provision, which states that parents, or the public agency may refer a child for special education evaluations. A parent should always ask for the evaluation in writing.

2. "You think your son needs to be tested for special education because he is struggling academically. We will think about it and let you know."

Parents have difficulty asking for initial evaluations because they do not know the correct language, and do not understand the importance of formally requesting testing for special education. Parents should ask, in writing, for a comprehensive case study evaluation, to be completed, by the school personnel. A comprehensive case study evaluation includes the following:

a. A medical history, on the child, done by the school nurse

b. A family and child history, that is usually completed, by the school social worker.

c. Psychological, educational, functional, and developmental testing, (done by the school psychologist). This should include more than one evaluation tool, an IQ test, academic levels, functional levels, and developmental levels if the child is between the ages of three to five, and educational levels if the child is over five.

d. An adaptive behavior scale, which evaluates the child's social skills, activities of daily living, other areas. Most schools use an adaptive behavior scale called the Vineland. If your child is older, I would recommend the Scale of Independent Behavior, which goes into areas that affect older children. All adaptive behavior scales are done by asking parents questions, (about what their child is able to do and not do) and the results are scored by the test giver, who is usually the school social worker. Pro Ed's Website is: **www.proedinc.com.**

e. Additional testing (may be done by related service personnel). For example: this testing might include a speech therapy evaluation, a occupational therapy evaluation, a physical therapy evaluation, and any other related services the child needs. Make sure that the therapists recommend amount of minutes of direct service in their report, after the testing is done. Several years ago school personnel in my area, pressured therapists to not include the amount of minutes in their reports. This tactic forces parents to bring up the subject.

f. Response to behavioral challenges. If the child exhibits behavior that negatively affects his education, make sure the school conducts a functional behavioral analysis, and write a positive behavior plan. A functional behavioral assessment is a process, which shows what a child is receiving by doing the negative behavior. When my daughter was younger, she would throw a temper tantrum any time she had to do academics. School personnel did believe that Angelina was trying to avoid the academics by throwing a temper tantrum. I was the one who finally figured out that she was misbehaving because the academics were too difficult. Decreasing, her academic time, helped dramatically improve her behavior.

School personnel not agreeing to evaluate

If school personnel decide not to test your child, despite your concerns and referral, they must give you prior written notice (PWN) according to IDEA 2004. This notice must describe what action they want to take or what action they refuse to take (in this case, their refusal to conduct a case study evaluation on your child), and explain why school personnel refused to take action, describe what factors the school used to make their decision. A parent has the option of getting an independent evaluation, to prove that their child has a disability; and then bringing it to the school district. The parent could also file for a due process hearing, and use the independent evaluation, as evidence that their child has a disability.

Some school districts have IEP meetings to determine what tests are going to be performed . These are commonly called "domain meetings," and parents must be invited under IDEA 2004. Parents are an equal part of the IEP team that determine, what tests are done. School personnel may try, and talk parents out of comprehensive testing, even though the child needs it.

Below is an example of a letter to a school district, from a parent, asking for an initial case study evaluation.

Name of School District Representative
Name of School District
Address
City, State and Zip Code
                                    Date

Dear

My name is Mary Johnson and I am the mother of Claudia Johnson. Claudia just started third grade and attends Mills Elementary School. Her date of birth is XX. I have been concerned about Claudia's inability to keep up academically with her peers, since she started school in first grade. Many times, I verbally asked that Claudia be tested for learning disabilities, but I never received a response. I am now formally, in writing, requesting a comprehensive case study evaluation to determine if Claudia is eligible for special education services, due to a learning disability or perhaps other undiagnosed disabilities. I am also asking for testing to determine if Claudia has an auditory processing disorder. This evaluation needs to include testing for learning disabilities, psychological and educational testing, an adaptive behavior scale, an IQ test, testing for auditory processing disorder, and medical and family histories. The reason I am asking for testing, is because Claudia is far behind her peers, in all areas of academics, as shown by her district-and-state-wide testing. There is also a long family history of learning disabilities. I expect to receive a response within ten school days, to set up an IEP (domain) meeting where the testing can be discussed.

Mary Johnson

Address

City, State, and Zip Code

The letter should include the child's name, school, grade, date of birth, and reasons that the parent is asking for the testing, and any specific testing the parent feels that their child needs. I found a wonderful *Learning Disabilities Checklist* from the National Center for Learning Disabilities. This checklist, can be found, at the Website **www.LD.org.**

Hand deliver, the letter to the special education office or your local special education cooperative; wherever the offices for special education in your district are. If you cannot hand deliver the request, send it via certified mail with a return receipt. If the school district does not respond, within ten days, write them again.

Name of School District Representative

Name of School District

Address

City, State and Zip Code

Date

Dear

I am writing this letter today because I did not receive a written response to the letter I sent to you on DATE. I gave the letter to your secretary, Margie. My letter of DATE was my formal request for a case study evaluation for my daughter Claudia Johnson. I stated my reasons for requesting the testing, to determine if my daughter is eligible for special education. I believe that Claudia may have a learning disability. IDEA 2004, requires that you notify me within ten days, of whether the school district will conduct a case study evaluation on my child, as I asked. As of this date, I have not received this notification. I hope this is an oversight on your part, and I hope to hear from you within five days. If I receive no response within the five days, I will have to consider filing a complaint with the state board of education.

Mary Johnson

Address

City, State and Zip Code

Chapter 2 contains an example of a letter to file a complaint with your state board of education.

Never tell school personnel something, that you have no intention of doing. For Example: Only tell school personnel that you will be filing a complaint, if you intend to. In the above scenario, the last line of the letter could state instead: *"If I* *do not receive a written response from you within five days, I will be **considering** filing a complaint with the state board of education."*

3. "We received your request for a case study evaluation for your child, come to this meeting, tomorrow, and let us professionals decide what testing your child needs."

Parents are equal members of the IEP team, and have the right to have input on any thing affecting their child. IDEA 2004 does now require that school districts discuss any information brought by the parent. School personnel cannot determine what testing the child needs; without parental input.

I suggest that you talk to other parents that have children with disabilities, and perhaps bring one to the meeting with you. Parents, who have been through the special education system, can often help parents that are new to the system. Pro-Ed is a publisher of tests and other materials that parents may use as a resource. They also offer autism rating scales as well as ADHD Rating Scales. The name is Pro-Ed. They can be reached at 1-800-897-3202 or Online at **www.proedinc.com.** A lot of times, when I am asking for testing for a child, I will ask for a specific test. That is why Pro-Ed is a great resource for parents, of available tests. Once the tests, are agreed upon by parents and school personnel, parents must sign a consent form. Consent forms, will be discussed later in this chapter.

IDEA 2004 requires that school districts send parents a ten day written notice, of all meetings. This notice must include a list of all the people who will be attending the meeting. If a parent agrees to a meeting before ten days, then they may waive the ten day written notice. The meeting is supposed to be held, at a "mutually convenient" time, for both parties.

4. "Please sign this blanket medical release form so that we can receive your child's medical records. We need the medical records before we can begin the evaluation."

A child's medical records are confidential. **Never sign a consent form to release medical records**. If there is a specific record, the school is interested in, obtain a copy of the medical record, check it for accuracy and only release it if you feel that it is in the best interest of your child--not the school. I have been shocked over the years, to find the strangest things in medical records; some of which actually work against children with disabilities. Schools are not entitled to medical records, no matter what they say, This, is another intimidation tactic. Parents must have the strength to stand up against this sort of intimidation, for the good of their child.

5. "Sign this blank consent form and we will fill in the educational and psychological tests later."

IDEA 2004 requires that school districts obtain **informed consent** from parents of the child; before conducting an evaluation. In order for a parent to give informed consent; the parent must understand what tests they are agreeing to. Parents should not sign a blank consent form. If an educator hands you a blank consent form to sign, hand it back to them and tell them to write in the testing before you sign. Remind them, of the changes brought about by IDEA 2004; specifically those concerning parent's rights to informed consent.

School personnel are required to use more than one test or measure to determine if a child has a disability and educational needs.

6. "Thank you for signing the consent form for the testing for your child. We will get back to you when we finish. Please be patient; it may take some time because other children are to be tested before your child."

IDEA 2004 requires that school districts finish case study evaluations within sixty days of parents signing the consent form. School districts, are not allowed, to have "lines" of children waiting for testing; that is illegal under IDEA 2004.

I once worked with a mother who only spoke Spanish. The school district told her, that her son would have to wait one and one half years, before he could be tested, to determine if he had a disability. In, my opinion, the school district personnel took advantage of the fact that the mother did not speak English. I became involved and worked with her (through an interpreter), so that her son could be tested, in a timely manner, to determine if he had a disability.

After the tests are completed, the school district will send you a ten day written notice to attend an IEP meeting, where your child's eligibility for special education will be discussed. The notice is required to list the meeting dates and time, and all of the people who will be at the meeting, and the reason for the meeting. The meeting, will probably be attended, by your child's teacher, principal, school psychologist, special education coordinator, and any related service personnel

Eligibility for Special Education

A child is eligible for special education if he or she meets two criterion;
a. The child has a disability.
b. The disability negatively affects the child's education. In other words the child has educational needs.

The eligibility conference will discuss all of the evaluations performed on your child, plus any information that you bring to the meeting. After all of the evaluation results are discussed, your child's eligibility will be discussed next. If your child has a disability, has educational needs, then the disability negatively affects their education, and they are eligible.

If the school district finds that your child does not have a disability, or that the disability does not affect his or her education, and you disagree, you have a couple of options. I would recommend getting an independent educational evaluation (IEE), taking it to the school district, and see if they will reconsider. If they refuse, then you may have to file for a due process hearing. But, do not give up, your child is depending on you!

Lies About Eligibility

1. "Your child does have a disability but we do not believe that his or her disability affects their education, or that your child has any educational needs."

I know a parent who has a son that was diagnosed with Pervasive Developmental Disorder (PDD). To this day, her school district states that his disability, doesn't negatively affect his education; even though they threatened to hold him back a couple of times, because he was failing in all academic areas. If the testing shows that your child's academics are below grade and age level, then their disability does affect their education, and they are eligible for special education services. Also, if your child has behavior that affects their ability to learn, then their disability is also affecting their education, and they would also be eligible for special education services. IDEA 2004 states that a child with a disability must receive a free appropriate public education even though they progress from grade to grade. This, is a great addition that will help children with disabilities, and their parents.

2. "Yes the testing showed your child is one year behind his peers, but in our district, a child with disabilities must be two years behind to qualify for special education services."

IDEA 2004, does not state that a child has to be two years behind, to qualify for special education services. All that it requires is that a child has a disability, has educational needs, and the needs negatively affect the child's education. When school personnel say things, that parents think might be lies, parents must question them, and stand up to them. I would ask the school personnel to "Please show me where in IDEA 2004 it states that a child must be two years behind, before they are eligible for special education services." There have been times, when I have had to get out my IDEA and state regulations, at an IEP meeting, and ask the school personnel to show me where that is found. In most cases, the school personnel were not able to find any reference to what they stated. **Parents must stand up to them!**

3. "Boy, we are so surprised that your child tested so low in all academic areas! But we don't really believe it, so don't worry about it."

In my over fifteen years of advocacy experience, I believe that most school psychologists, have the ability, to evaluate children with disabilities. Where I disagree with them on, is how they **interpret** the test scores. If a child is tested, and the test results show below age and grade level academics, then the child needs appropriate educational services to bring their academics up to grade appropriate levels. This, is called, remediation. In my opinion, school personnel sometimes state that they do not "believe" low test scores, because they do not want to provide additional educational services. Parents need to be assertive and make sure that the school district is addressing every area that is below grade and age level. (Don't forget functional areas as well as academic areas).

Pam and Peter Wright in *From Emotions to Advocacy*, give instructions on how to make graphs of test scores. This is an excellent skill to learn, that you will use many times; especially if you go to a due process hearing. I brought my son's test scores, put on a graph, to an IEP meeting. The school personnel, in my opinion, could not try and gloss over the results; because they could see them in black and white.

Lies about Reevaluations

1. "The IEP team had a meeting and decided not to reevaluate your child. You wouldn't want to put your child through that, would you?"

If a meeting was held, without your knowledge, file a complaint with your state board of education. The complaint should state that your school district violated IDEA 2004 by having an illegal meeting; because they failed to invite you. The resolution to the complaint, is that any decisions made at that meeting is null and void (like it never happened).

IDEA 2004, requires that a child with disabilities, be reevaluated every three years, unless parents and school personnel agree, that a reevaluation is not needed. IDEA 2004 also states a school district must reevaluate the child, if the educational needs change, or if the parent requests it. Most school personnel do not tell parents, that they have the right to ask for a reevaluation. If you believe your child, needs to be, reevaluated bring it up in an IEP meeting (also, make sure it is in the meeting notes). Another option would be to request the reevaluation formally in writing, and ask that the consent form be sent to you within a few days. Remember do not sign a blank evaluation consent form!

2. "We have enough information to determine if your child needs to be reevaluated. We are not interested in any information you can bring."

IDEA 2004 adds a section that states that school personnel must review evaluations and information, provided by the parents of the child. This is an exciting addition, that will help children with disabilities and their parents. Parents should also be sure that they are given copies, of their child's district and state wide testing scores, every time they are taken. These could be used later, if a dispute arises with your school district.

After the review by the school district and parents, the team is to decide if any additional information is needed, to determine the following:

a. Whether the child's disability continues.

b. The educational needs of the child.

c. Present levels of **academic achievement, functional achievement**, and related developmental needs of the child.

d.. Whether the child's disability, negatively affects his or her education.

e. Whether the child needs, (or continues to need) special education services, to benefit from their education.

 f. Whether any changes should be made, to the educational and related services that the child needs. Parents need to ask for the educational and related services testing that their child needs. After the evaluation is finished, a determination is made by the IEP team about whether a child has a disability, and whether the disability negatively affects the education. If this is true, then the child continues to be eligible for special education services.

School districts also misinterpret test scores for reevaluations. If the child scored poorly, educators often say they don't "believe" the results. Parents need to be certain that their child receives special education services for every area that they tested below grade and age appropriate levels including social skills and activities of daily living.

Chapter 5: Independent Educational Evaluations and Independent Educational Evaluations at Public Expense

Parents need to understand what an independent educational evaluation (IEE) is, before they can begin to over come educator's lies. An independent educational evaluation or is an educational evaluation, for a child with a disability, conducted by a qualified person, who does not work for the school district. Independent educational evaluations are initiated, and paid for by parents (though school districts can be asked to reimburse the parent, after the evaluation is done). Parents get IEEs for many reasons:

 a. To determine what the child's disability is, especially if school personnel state that a child does not have a disability or if the parent thinks that their child may have an undiagnosed disability.

b. To determine what academic, developmental or functional level a child is at.

c. To figure out what educational, related, or functional services a child needs.

d. To convince school personnel, that a child requires an increase in educational or related services. This is used, often when a child requires more therapy or educational services; which school district personnel refuse to give.

e. So that a child with disabilities can receive an appropriate educational placement

The best way to find an independent evaluator is to ask other parents of children with disabilities, call a disability organization, or contact a parent training and information center (see Easy-To-Understand Definitions). There is a list of all PTICs in Pam and Peter Wright's book *From Emotions to Advocacy* . The most important information to find out when looking for an independent evaluator is:

a. Whether they are qualified to perform the evaluation.

b. Whether or not, this person is a current or past employee, of a school district. If the independent evaluator is a past employee of a school district, talk to them, before you make a decision about whether to use them or not. A past school district employee may be biased against children with disabilities, and their parents; but you will not know until you talk to them.

c. Whether or not the evaluator, is willing to complete a comprehensive report; that states **specifically** what special education and related services, a child needs, and the amount of time per week that the child needs the service.

Check out your state board of education's Web site; they may have information about independent evaluators. Be careful though, it is possible that the evaluators on the list, may be current or past school district personnel. The really good, independent evaluators in my state of Illinois, are not all on the state board of education's list of independent evaluators. If a parent gets an IEE for their child, and the school district includes the recommendations from the IEE on the child's IEP, parents should ask for reimbursement of the IEE. A lot of parents that I know, do not ask for reimbursement of the IEE, because they are happy as long as school personnel include the recommendations in their child's IEP. If parents don't ask school personnel for reimbursement, they will never know if school personnel would have reimbursed them.

Lies about Independent Evaluations

1. "Why would you go and get an independent evaluation? Our school psychologist is wonderful and wants what is best for your child."

IDEA 2004 states that school districts do not have to provide the "best" education for your child, just what is "appropriate." In some cases, school personnel, are biased against giving a child with disabilities, an appropriate education. This means that parents must do everything within their power, to see that their child is educated appropriately. This may mean an IEE or even a due process hearing.

2. "We don't have to accept this outside evaluation that you brought. Besides this person, is not as qualified as our school psychologist."

IDEA 2004 requires that school district personnel must "consider" any information brought to them by the parents; this includes IEEs. As long as the person who conducted the IEE, meets state and federal standards for their profession, then they are considered qualified, by the state In a due process hearing that I advocated at, the special education coordinator stated that their school psychologist was more qualified to perform educational testing on children with disabilities, than a clinical psychologist. (A clinical psychologist has a doctorate degree, which is not required for a school psychologist). I just rolled my eyes and hoped that the hearing officer didn't believe it; which he did not.

Standards for different professions, may be found, on your state board of education's Website. If they are not available, contact your state board of education.

3. "This diagnosis of autism is a medical diagnosis and we do not have to accept a medical diagnosis."

I have heard this numerous times. Medical diagnoses, are accepted by school districts--as long as the medical diagnosis negatively affects the child's education.

School districts often do not want to recognize and label a child with autism. This forces parents to seek an independent evaluation with an autism specialist. As long as the IEE, is written in a way that states that the disability, that the child has affects his or her education, it doesn't matter if the specialist is a medical doctor or not. Doctors must often be reminded, to write any report in educational terms, not medical terms. Educators may fuss if a parent brings an IEE that diagnoses a child with autism, but they usually back down if a parent is "assertively persistent. " It is important for parents and school personnel, to understand what the child's disability is, before they can decide what special education services the child needs. I deal with children a lot, that have undiagnosed disabilities. This makes it difficult to determine what their educational needs are. Parents must investigate and make sure that their child's disability label is appropriate for their child.

4. "We cannot give your child the special education service that is on this IEE, because we do not offer that service."

A child with disabilities is entitled to FAPE from age three to twenty one; with educational and related services that they need, to benefit from their education. States are allowed, to make their own decisions about education from 18-21; check with your state board of education and state rules to see what their rules are.

IDEA 2004 does not allow school districts to pick-and-choose which special education services they are going to provide. If the school cannot provide a service your child needs, then they can find and pay an outside professional, to provide that service. Schools are reluctant to do this, but this is where parents must be "assertively persistent."

IEEs at Public Expense

IDEA 2004 states that parents have the right to an independent educational evaluation at public expense, **if they disagree with the school districts evaluation.** In IDEA 2004 300.502 it states that school personnel may ask the parent the reasons why they object to the schools evaluation; but they may not require the parent to give an explanation. IDEA 2004 states that parents are entitled to only one IEE at public expense, after each evaluation that they disagree with. Several areas of disagreement may be included in one IEE. If the school district conducts an evaluation in several different areas (for example academic difficulty, occupational therapy, speech therapy, etc), the parent would be entitled to an IEE for the entire evaluation; in all the areas tested; that the parent disagrees with.

This doesn't mean, that parents cannot pay for additional IEEs, whenever they think it is necessary, it simply restricts the number of IEEs at public expense.

Parents have the right under FERPA to review and receive copies of "education records." "Included in these "records" are test instruments, question booklets, answer sheets, evaluations, surveys, inventories, and other materials that identify a student by name, and are maintained by the district." This information came from a policy letter by OSEP dated September 13, 2005. Many parents want access to the testing "protocols," for their child, so that they can be examined by the independent evaluator, for accuracy, or used in a due process hearing.

Parents should also include any qualifications they want the evaluator to have, any waiver of criteria asking for, and any specific tests they want included in the evaluation. At one of the due process hearings that I advocated at, for an IEE at public expense; the hearing officer wanted to know if the mother had notified the school district of what part of the evaluation that she disagreed with. Luckily, I had advised the mother to put the reasons for her disagreement in the IEE request letter. Below is a copy of a letter requesting an IEE at Public Expense:

Name of School Representative
Name of School District
Address
City, State, and Zip Code

Date

Dear

This letter is to formally request, an independent educational evaluation at public expense for my daughter, Justine Miller, who is in eighth grade. Justine has been eligible for special education services, since second grade under the disability category of learning disability. Justine's full scale IQ in second grade was 104. When Justine was reevaluated in fifth grade her full scale IQ, had dropped to 84. When Justine was recently re evaluated her IQ, had dropped further to 74. That means that according to the school districts testing, Justine's IQ has dropped a total of 30 points, in six years. Justine is also at least three years academically behind her grade and age appropriate peers, as shown by her state-and-district-wide testing. According to many experts in special education, a child's IQ only drops because of a traumatic brain injury or an inappropriate education. Since Justine has not had a traumatic brain injury, I believe that the education she is receiving for her learning disabilities is not appropriate to meet her educational needs. Justine needs an independent educational evaluation at public expense, to determine if and why her IQ dropped, and what educational and special education services she needs to receive FAPE. I am requesting an evaluation with a clinical psychologist, due to the thirty point drop in Justine's IQ. A clinical psychologist is qualified to determine if and why Justine's I.Q. has dropped, but also what her educational and special education service needs are. I am also asking for a waiver of cost criteria, due to the fact, that a clinical psychologist charges more than a school psychologist. I believe that due to the thirty point drop in IQ, and Justine's three year academic delay, this requires a waiver of cost criteria.

According to IDEA 2004, the school district has two choices after receiving a request for an independent educational evaluation at public expense. Either they can pay for the evaluation, or they can file for a due process hearing. I expect to hear from you within ten days, with the school districts decision.

Mary Miller

Address

City, State, and Zip Code

The Office of Special Education (OSEP), allows school districts to make criteria for IEEs at public expense; "**but only if it does not prevent a parent from getting an independent educational evaluation**." Parents must also be able to ask for waivers if the child's disability warrants it.

I learned about the two reasons that a child's IQ drops, from a clinical psychologist, who testified for a child I was advocating for at due process. I believe that this psychologist's testimony helped me win an IEE at public expense for this young man. According to the schools testing the young man's IQ had dropped thirty points; and there did not appear to be any reason for it, other than an inappropriate education.

Lies about IEEs at Public Expense

1. "The school district received your request for an independent evaluation at public expense. You must file for a due process hearing to receive one."

IDEA 2004 states that once a school district receives a request for an IEE at public expense they have two choices:

a. Pay for the IEE at public expense; or

b. File for a due process hearing, to prove to a hearing officer that their schools evaluation is appropriate. The evaluation also includes the schools interpretation of test results, which I often disagree with. If school personnel do not respond to a parent's request for an IEE at public expense, the parent may end up having to file for a due process hearing to prove to a hearing officer that their child needs the IEE at public expense.

2. "Our school will pay for the IEE at public expense but we get to decide which tests are done."

Parents and school personnel must agree on the areas that are to be tested, but not the tests themselves. If an agreement cannot be reached, on the areas to be tested, then the school district must file for a due process hearing. If they do not file for a due process hearing, then the parent will unfortunately have to--if they want the IEE at public expense.

3. "We will pay for the IEE at public expense but you must choose an evaluator from our list."

On February 20, 2004 the Office of Special Education Programs (OSEP), published a policy letter regarding IEEs at public expense. This letter was an answer to a letter received by Alice D. Parker, Ed.D. from the California

Department of Education. Dr. Parker wanted to know if ". . .it is permissible for a public agency to restrict a parent's choice of an IEE to only the evaluators on a list provided the parent by the public agency and whether the public agency has the ultimate authority to choose the evaluator". OSEPs response was "**It is the parent, not the district, who has the right to choose which evaluator . . . will conduct the evaluation.**" Parts of this letter, will be printed, at the end of this chapter. The entire letter, can also be found on the Website **www.ed.gov.** Type in, special education policy letters. The letter can be found, in the first quarter section of 2004.

Parents should check out the Office of Special Education's policy letters, at the above website, to see if any apply to their child. While looking through the policy letters, I was able to find some information on behavior, discipline, and manifestation determination decisions; that I could use in my advocacy.

I already mentioned, that I advocated at a due process hearing, for an IEE at public expense. The school district handed the mother a list of three evaluators and said pick one. I felt very strongly that IDEA (which was in effect at the time), did not allow school personnel to pick the evaluator; but left the evaluator choice to the parent. After checking the names on the list, all three of the names, were past or retired school district personnel; which we believe made them biased, against the child. The mother ended up filing for a due process hearing; which I advocated at, and won. Unfortunately, I found the letter from OSEP about IEE's at public expense after the due process; or I would have used it in my case.

4. "The evaluator that you get; must meet our cost, geographical, and professional qualifications."

School district personnel are allowed to make criteria (such as those controlling the geographical, cost and professional qualifications), as long as these criteria do not prevent a parent from getting an IEE at public expense. If a parent wants the school district to waive these criteria, they must ask the school district for a waiver, and show reasons, why this is warranted.

In the due process that I advocated at, for an IEE at public expense, the hearing officer ruled that because the child's IQ had dropped thirty points the mother was entitled to a waiver of the IEE criteria in the area of cost and credentials. Another of the criteria that I asked a waiver for, was geographic. We live in a fairly small town, with few qualified independent evaluators. The mother found a great evaluator, but he was out of the geographic and cost limits that the school district imposed. The hearing officer ruled, that the criteria the school district set up prevented the mom from receiving an IEE at public expense, and ordered that the evaluation be performed, by the evaluator chosen by the mother.

Below is parts of the OSEP letter about IEE's at Public Expense

Alice D. Parker, Ed.D.

Assistant Superintendent   Stamped Feb 20, 2004

California Department of Education

721 Capitol Mall

Sacramento, California 94244

Dear Dr. Parker:

This is a response to your letter to Larry Ringer, Associate Division Director, Monitoring and State Improvement Planning, requesting guidance from the Office of Special Education Programs (OSEP) regarding an independent education evaluation (IEE) under 34 CFR 300.502 of the regulations implementing the Individuals with Disabilities Education Act (IDEA). Specifically, you ask whether it is permissible for a public agency to restrict a parent's choice of an IEE to only the evaluators on a list provided the parent by the public agency and whether the public agency has the ultimate authority to choose the evaluator.

The current IDEA regulations specify that the right of a parent to obtain an IEE is triggered if the parent disagrees with an evaluation initiated by a public agency. See 300.502 (b)(1). The regulations also require that on request for an IEE, a public agency must provide the parent information about where an IEE may be obtained, and the agency crityeria applicable for IEEs. 34 CFR300.502a)(2) and (e)(1). The public agency must set criteria under which an IEE can be obtained at public expense, including the location of the evaluation, and the qualifications of the examiner. . . Other than establishing these criteria, a public agency may not impose conditions or timelines related to a parent obtaining an IEE at public expense. See 300.502(e)(2).

It is not inconsistent with IDEA for a district to publish a list of the names and addresses of evaluators that meet agency criteria, including reasonable cost criteria. This can be an effective way for agencies to inform parents of how and where they may obtain an IEE. **In order to ensure the parent's right to an independent evaluation, it is the parent, not the district, who has the right to choose which evaluator on the list will conduct the IEE. . .Therefore, when enforcing IEE criteria, the district must allow parents the opportunity to select an evaluator who is not on the list but who meets the criteria set by the public agency.**

In addition, when enforcing IEE criteria, the district must allow parents the opportunity to demonstrate that unique circumstances justify the selection of an evaluator that does not meet agency criteria.

Section 300.502(b)(2) of the regulations state that "If a parent requests and IEE at public expense, the public agency must, without unnecessary delay, either (i) initiate a hearing under 300.507 to show that its evaluation is appropriate; or (ii)ensure that an independent educational evaluation is provided at public expense, unless the agency demonstrates in a hearing under 300.507 that the evaluation obtained by the parent did not meet agency criteria.. ."

Sincerely

Stephanie Smith Lee

Director Office of Special Education Programs

Chapter 6: Individual Education Plans

After a child is found eligible, for special education, the IEP team (which includes the parents) will have a meeting to write the child's IEP. The thing that parents need to remember, is the plan should be individualized, to meet their child's unique educational needs; caused by their disability. A child's IEP must be reviewed, at least yearly. IDEA 2004 has allowed fifteen states to participate in a Multi year IEP project (three year). Parents should opt out of this project, which they are allowed to do.

Now I will be discussing the contents of the IEP. One of the reasons that I wanted to include this, is because school district personnel may try and skip over some important parts of the IEP. Once parents know what should be in an IEP, they can bring up any areas that the educators may leave out.

An IEP must contain the following:

a. Sign in sheet for participants of the IEP meeting.

b. A copy of the meeting notice, with names of all people who will attend.

c. A review of the child's academic progress. IDEA 2004 now requires that schools discuss any lack of expected progress, and parent concerns, which may allow parents to have more input at their child's IEP meeting.

d. An analysis of the strengths of the student.

e. An analysis of the weaknesses of the student.

f Present levels of **academic achievement** and **functional performance,** for all children with disabilities. Before IDEA 2004, schools were required to put present levels of educational performance. Functional performance was never included before IDEA 2004. Knowing functional levels is important for children with cognitive disabilities (mental retardation), and also children with other disabilities, that require life skill training. Once a parent knows a child's functional level, they can address whether they need services in that area; and if goals should be written.

g. Information about how your child's progress, will be measured, and how you will be notified.

h. A section on whether the child's behavior, interferes with his or her learning. Parents need to be careful about this one. School personnel sometimes put no on the IEP, and then when the child has behavior problems, they suspend them from school. If the child has behavior difficulties, school personnel should conduct a functional behavioral analysis (FBA), and write a positive behavioral plan..

i. A section on whether assistive technology, is needed for a student to access his or her education. In my experience, some school personnel misinterpret this section to mean "Does the child receive assistive technology?" If the student doesn't, this section may be skipped over. Assistive Technology can make the difference between failing and succeeding for children with disabilities.

j. A section on whether a child is blind or deaf, and requires Braille or communication support.

k. IDEA 2004 requires, that schools only write short term objectives, for children with disabilities who take alternate assessments; instead of all children with disabilities, as required previously. Schools must continue to include a "statement of measurable annual goals." for all children with disabilities. Remember, academic as well as functional goals need to be written; if your child needs it.

l. IDEA 2004 added a new section about "individual appropriate accommodations for taking district-and-state-wide assessments.

IDEA 2004 now states that **all children with disabilities are included in all state-and-district-wide assessment programs,** unless the IEP team decides that the testing is inappropriate.

m. A description of any transition services a child may need, and a transition plan. IDEA 2004 changed the age this is done, from fourteen to sixteen years of age, unless the IEP team determines that it needs to be done earlier.

Also, at least one year prior to the child turning eighteen; the IEP team must inform the child of rights that will transfer to them when they reach the age of majority (eighteen years of age).

n. IDEA 2004, states that IEPs must now have a section on "anticipated needs". This would be a great time for parents to give input on what they see as their child's "anticipated needs."

o. A list of special education and related services that your child may need, to benefit from their education. This section should very specifically contain all the special education services your child is to receive, including the amount of minutes that they will be receiving this service.

According to the NICHCY document *Developing Your Child's IEP*, Related services can include, but are not limited to, any of the following:

Assistive Technology	Physical Therapy
Audiology	**Psychological Services**
Counseling Services	Recreation
Early Identification	Rehabilitation Counseling
Medical Services	School Health Services
Occupational Therapy	Social Work Services in Schools
Orientation and Mobility Services	Speech-Language Pathology
Parent Counseling/Training	Transportation

IDEA 2004 added a new section that states that the IEP now needs to address whether the special education and related services "are based on peer reviewed research." IDEA 2004 also includes new language about research-based-instruction, which requires that there is research to prove that the curriculum works for children to learn.

p. Educational placement of the child for the next school year. According to IDEA 2004, placement should not be discussed until the child's educational needs, program, and goals are developed. Placement must be in the least restrictive environment (LRE). LRE is defined as "to the maximum extent appropriate, children with disabilities. . .are educated with children without disabilities, and not further excluded. The IEP must also include the amount of time a child with a disability is in the regular classroom, with their non-disabled peers. School personnel also must give a child Supplementary Aids and Services to allow them to participate in the regular classroom. From the NICHCY document, *Developing your child's IEP* "Some examples of these additional services and supports are: a. adapted equipment, b. assistive technology, training for staff, student, and/or parents c. peer tutors, d. a one-on-one aide, e. adapted materials and f. collaboration/consultation among staff, parents, and/or other professionals. The IEP team must really work together to make sure your child gets the supplementary aids and services that he or she needs to be successful." These aids and services must also be given to the child for extracurricular and non academic activities.

q. Any modifications that the child requires to the regular education curriculum.

r. Anticipated date of graduation. Parents need to remember that children with disabilities are entitled to be educated through the age of twenty-one years of age not eighteen years of age. Check with your state board of education to see what your states rules are.

s. Whether the child needs extended school year services, to benefit from their education.

t. An eligibility sheet stating that your child is eligible for special education services, or not. Read this sheet carefully!

u. A separate eligibility determination sheet, that has the criteria for determining if a child has a certain disability. Each disability category has their own eligibility sheet.

v. Reports of any evaluations or reevaluations performed on your child.

Also, if a parent input statement is written, make certain that it is attached to the IEP. If a parent usually attends an IEP alone, consider bringing a friend or an educational advocate, and a tape recorder. I do believe that more intimidation occurs at IEP meetings, if the parent is alone; no witnesses I guess.

Three model forms were developed by OSEP, as required in IDEA 2004. The forms are Prior Written Notice, IEP and Procedural Safeguards. Copies of these forms can be found at: **http://idea.ed.gov.** In the box, type in special education model forms.

LIES ABOUT IEP MEETINGS

1. "If you are planning on bringing someone with you, you must notify us (the school district) at least five days before the meeting."

Parents do not have to notify school personnel, if they are bringing someone to an IEP meeting. If I am going to an IEP meeting with a parent, I tell them not to notify the school that I am coming. Sometimes, surprise is the best advocacy tool there is. I have been in meetings, where the school did not know I was coming, and there were not enough chairs. I said "No problem. We will wait until you get some," and we waited until they went and got a few more chairs. I was recently in an IEP meeting where the room was so small, I was practically sitting on top of the child's teacher. The mother mentioned after the meeting, that the school has many larger rooms, and did not understand why they used such a small room. In my opinion, things like this are intimidation tactics, which I usually ignore.

2. "We left you a chair at the end of the table."

Parents can sit anywhere they want to! If possible, sit next to the person who is in charge of writing the IEP, so that you can check and see what they are writing, and make suggestions. I often say during a meeting, "Write that down, because it is important." One time, I had the opportunity to attend an IEP meeting with a special education attorney. He loved when I kept asking them what they were writing. He finally said, "JoAnn why don't you go sit by the person writing the IEP so that you do not have to keep getting up." I followed his advice, and sat next to the person writing the IEP. He told me after the meeting, that he had never used that technique. I felt great! I taught a special education attorney an advocacy technique!

3. "We don't really need to hear from you (the parent)! We have all the information we need. Trust us, we have more experience."

Parents are equal partners in the IEP meeting. They are a required part of the IEP team that determines what special education services their child receives. According to NICHCY's *A Parents Guide: Developing Your Child's IEP*. "Parents have a job to do at the IEP. . .The parents' job at the IEP meeting is to:

a. Learn and understand the process.

b. Share information,

c. Ask questions.

d. Offer suggestions.

e. Keep the teams focus on the big picture and your child's long- term needs.

 f. Speak up on your child's behalf".

Parents also need to take notes. Don't forget to ask the person speaking to either slow down, or explain what they are talking about. I am amazed when I go to an IEP meeting with a new parent (one who is new to the special education process), and the parent does not ask for explanations of terms they do not know. I usually take them out in the hall, and tell them that they need to ask the person speaking for an explanation; so that they can understand what is going on and be an equal participant in the IEP process.

4. "I am sorry; your child's IEP is already written and we can't add anything to it, but we really appreciate your input."

I am often asked by parents, if school districts are allowed to bring a pre-written IEP, to the IEP meeting. The answer is yes, but school personnel should be willing to send a copy of the "proposed" IEP to the parent, before the meeting; and be willing to change anything the parent does not agree to. The parent will probably have to write a letter to the school district, and ask for a copy of the IEP before the meeting. The parent should tell school personnel that they need a copy of the "proposed" IEP before the meeting, so that they will be prepared to be an active participant. If the "proposed" IEP has something that you disagree with, ask that it be changed or taken out. I have had this experience myself with something pre written that I disagreed with. The person doing the writing crossed out the disagreed item, had the parent initial it, and then wrote what I asked them too. I am not saying that they did not fuss--but they ultimately did it. Parents' absolutely must speak up when they disagree with something written in their child's IEP. That is why I suggested sitting next to the person writing the IEP, so that they can tell the person that they disagreed with it, and hopefully they will change it, or at least put that the parent disagrees.

Most educators are professional enough, to at least listen to a parent's input, but not all will. But, this is a great opportunity to speak up and give it to them anyway! I call that "assertive persistence!" If they still refuse to add anything to the IEP, or change something, stop the meeting, get a copy of what has already been done, leave and let them know that you will be considering, filing a complaint with your state board of education.

5. "The school cannot give your child that service because we have a waiting list for that service."

Waiting lists, are not allowed, under IDEA 2004. Children with disabilities have the right to educational and related services to meet their unique educational needs-- without waiting. If the school district cannot give your child a needed service, they must find an outside service provider who can, and they must pay for it.

6. "We don't care if you think your child needs Applied Behavioral Analysis! IDEA 2004 does not say that we have to provide this program?"

Applied Behavior Analysis (ABA), is often called the Lovaas method, after the person who developed it, Dr. Lovaas. ABA is a behavioral treatment that uses discrete trial teaching. ABA, has been extensively researched, and is usually used for young children with autism. For ABA to be effective, children should start as early as possible, preferably before the age of five. ABA requires very structured intensive one on one teaching for thirty five to forty hours per week. The teacher's assistant providing the ABA program, should have extensive training, and be under the supervision of a professional, who is experienced in applied behavior analysis. The individual child's program should be **designed,** by a professional in behavior analysis, with a masters or doctorate degree. The professional should also have experience in working with people with autism, and experience in behavior analysis. The professional is responsible for supervising the teacher assistants, and meeting with them on a regular basis (2-3 times a month) for training, and any changes that need to be made.

Information on ABA, can be found at the Website **www.lovaas.com.** ABA shows very good promise as a behavioral treatment for children with autism. A good book on ABA that can be purchased at **www.proedinc.com** is *Behavior Intervention For Young Children With Autism* which is edited by Catherine Maurice and Co edited by Gina Green and Stephen C. Luce.

IDEA 2004 says that children with disabilities have the right to a free appropriate public education, provided by the school district, free of charge. A lot of schools, do not want to provide ABA programs; which means that parents must file for a due process hearing. There are many ABA/Lovaas due process and court cases available on **www.wrightslaw.com.** Some parents start the ABA program at home, and then file for a due process hearing, for reimbursement. If a parent files for a due process hearing, stating that the schools proposed placement is not appropriate for their child, and that ABA is appropriate; it is easier to prove their case if the child is making progress in the ABA program. Burden of proof at due process will be discussed in Chapter 9.

7. "We don't think that your child needs extended school year (ESY) or assistive technology (AT). Besides those services cost too much, and we are a poor school district."

Many school districts bring up money when discussing special education and related services. Parents should never be expected, to worry about the districts budget; that is the school personnel's job. A parent's job, is to see that their child receives FAPE, that includes special education and related services to meet their child needs. Several years ago, I was advocating for a high school student who had severe learning disabilities. His mother and I were asking for a computer program (which the mother investigated herself), which cost $19.95. The mother felt that it would help her son increase his reading skills. I had to bring this up during an IEP meeting several times (because the educators kept trying to change the subject), before the special education coordinator, finally threw up his hands and said "Okay we will pay for it". I turned my head, looked him in the eye, smiled and said "Thank You". He gave a disgusted grunt; because he was not able to distract me from discussing the computer program. Remember REPEAT, REPEAT, REPEAT--and make sure anything agreed to, is in the IEP before you leave.

"Assistive Technology" (AT) can be something as simple as a large pen, which would make it easier for a child with cerebral palsy to grasp their pen better, or as complicated as an electronic communication device. In Illinois, we have the Illinois Assistive Technology program, which loans out assistive technology devices, so that parents can see if the particular device works for their child. More information including a funding manual, can be found at the Website **www.iltech.org** . Check with your state board of education to see if your state has the same type of program. Parents need to investigate and see if there is any assistive technology devices that would benefit their child's education; and bring it up at the IEP meeting.

"Extended School Year" (ESY) is a term to describe any special education and related services, which are given outside of the normal school year. For example, if a parent thought that their child needed math tutoring, in the summer, they could ask for it under the category of ESY. There have been several court cases and articles written about ESY. I have found, that there are several things that must be considered, to determine if a child is eligible for ESY: a. Regression and recoupment, the likelihood that the child would regress so much that it would take too long to relearn the skills. b. Nature and severity of the child's disability. c. Skills that have just been learned, by the child (emerging skills). d. Whether the child's behavior has affected their ability to learn e. Any special circumstances that applies to your child.

OSEP released a policy letter on ESY on February 4, 2003. The letter states "A public agency may not limit extended school year services to particular categories of disability, or unilaterally limit the type, amount, or duration of those services."

In my experience, most school personnel quickly go past the ESY section on the IEP; without really discussing whether the child needs it or not. If you think that you child needs ESY, mention it in your parent input statement, and make sure it is included in your child's IEP. If your school district does not offer these services, they must contract with another school district, or outside professionals to provide the services.

8. "You do not have the right to tell us what methodology to use to teach your child."

School personnel often tell parents that they cannot dictate what methodology school districts use. A new US District Court case KL vs. Mercer Island School District; states that the methodology, used by teachers, must be discussed at the IEP meeting, and placed in the child's IEP. As of the writing of this book, this case, has not been overturned (To my knowledge). This court ruling does give parents the opportunity to be involved in discussing teaching methodology used for their child.

In the *No Child Left Behind Parents Guide* it states that "Parents may be able to use this information to find out about the program and curricula selection at their child's school." This leads me to believe that parents do have the right to have input on the curriculum and methodology used to teach their child.

9. "We need your signature on the IEP, before we can start implementing it."

Parents often call and say, "I don't agree with my child's IEP so I told them I wouldn't sign it." IDEA 2004 does require a parent's signature for all evaluations and initial special education services. IDEA 2004 does state that parents must consent to special education services, but is not specific about how the school should get consent. I have heard from some parents, that some school districts, do ask the parent to sign the IEP, to show consent. Check with your state board of education, and see if your state requires, a parent to sign their child's IEP, to show consent for services. In Chapter 7 is an article from Wayne Steedman Esq. entitled *Ten Tips: How to Use IDEA 2004 to Improve Your Child's Special Education.* Wayne gives information on how to handle consent, if you only agree with parts of the IEP.

In the Supreme Court case *Schaffer v. Weast,* the judges ruled, that if parents do not agree to changes in the IEP, that the school district wants to make, it is the **responsibility** of the school district to file for a due process hearing. The reason this is important, is because, the burden of proof in some states, is on the party that filed. Also, in the past, parents were often forced to file for a due process hearing because the school wouldn't. This Supreme Court ruling, makes it clear, that school districts must file for a due process hearing, if the parents disagree with the proposed IEP. The Supreme Court got this one right! More on *Schaffer v. Weast* on burden of proof in chapter 9.

10. "We will send you a copy of the IEP when we are finished with it, probably in a few days."

Parents should **never** leave an IEP meeting without reading the IEP and getting a completed copy of the IEP. The IEP should be finished when the meeting is over, not later. If a parent does not get a copy of the IEP at the meeting, changes could be made without your knowledge or agreement. **READ IT!**

11. "I know that you are surprised that we want to change your child's placement; but IDEA 2004 doesn't say that we have to tell you in advance."

Actually, IDEA 2004 does require that school districts provide prior written notice (PWN), if they want to change a child's label, placement, or anything related to the child's education. The US Department of Education's IDEA 2004 Website **http://idea.ed.gov** states that this notice must include the following components:

a. It must define the changes that the school district wants to make (or refuses to make).

b. It must explain why the school proposed or refused to take action.

c. It must describe each evaluation, procedure, assessment, record, or report used as a basis for the proposed or refused action.

d. It must provide sources the parent can contact to obtain assistance, and describe other options considered, and why these options were rejected.

e. It must describe the factors that were relevant to the schools proposal or refusal.

If the parent disagrees with the proposed IEP, and the school district has not given PWN of the proposed changes, then the school must do so within ten days. Parents must insist that school districts give them PWN, if they want to make the changes described above. One of the good parts of prior written notice, is that school personnel must tell parents, what evaluations, or assessments they used in making this decision. I interpret this to mean, that school personnel must have evidence, before deciding to make changes; which has not always been the case, in the past.

If parents attend their child's IEP, and the school wants to make changes (in placement, label, or anything related to the child's education), they should insist on prior written notice, before they discuss the changes. I would tell school personnel that the meeting is over. I will wait until I receive PWN, then we can reconvene the IEP meeting, to discuss the changes. It is so sad that parents have to enforce IDEA 2004, but this is the reality!

Noncompliance with the IEP

I often get phone calls about what to do when a school district writes a great IEP--and then refuses to implement it. My advice is to immediately write a letter to the person in your district responsible for special education, and notify them that they are in non-compliance with your child's IEP. Noncompliance means that the school district is not following your child's IEP. Mention the specific violation, how you know about the violation, and what your evidence is of the violation. In the letter, state that you expect them to comply immediately with your child's IEP. Also, mention that you expect to receive a written response within five days. If the school district does not reply, or denies the violation, despite your evidence, file a complaint with your state board of education. A few years ago, I was a member of the OSEP advisory board in Illinois. Also on the board were several state board of education employees. I asked them what parents could do if the school district refused to comply with their child's IEP. They told me that the best way to handle it was to file a state complaint. Remember: Your child's IEP is part of the evidence. The rest of the evidence is how you found out that school personnel were not giving your child the services in his or her IEP. It is a terrible shame that parents must be the enforcement mechanism of IDEA 2004; but this is the real world!

Some last thoughts about IEPs

The IEP process is often adversarial, pitting school personnel against parents. Most parents that I know try to be professional, but at the same time advocate for needed educational services. You have already heard me say, "Be assertively persistent." But, sometimes the negative attitude of the educators prevents children from receiving what they need. I recently advocated for a ten year old boy with autism. His mom and I went to several IEP meetings, over several months, to try and get the boy the educational services that he needed. We received much resistance from his special education teacher. Over the summer, the mother and her children moved and changed school districts. When the young man started his new school, his mother called me, and stated that things were going very well. His new teacher worked hard to find a curriculum that would teach him to read. In two months, he made more progress in reading, than he did the last three years in the other school district. His teacher, also gave the young man, some individual instruction to help him in all areas of his academics. The teacher was also knowledgeable about autism, and behavioral issues associated with it. He also used a behavioral system that worked well. I was pleased that things were going so well.

I wish that I had a miracle solution to change some school personnel's attitudes, but unfortunately, I do not; My best advice is simply to "Just keep trying."

I would also like to mention, how important it is for a parent to tell educators when they are doing positive things to help your child.

Chapter 7: Free Appropriate Public Education

Free Appropriate Public Education, or FAPE, is one of the hardest concepts--for parents and school personnel alike--to understand. In fact, this term is so poorly defined, that the United States Supreme Court had to write a legal definition. The legal definition of FAPE is "Special education and related services that are designed to meet the child's unique needs, gives meaningful benefit, and has been given at no charge to the parents. FAPE includes an Individual Education Plan that is designed to meet the child's unique educational needs, and gives meaningful benefit". The first Supreme Court case, entitled *Board of Education vs. Rowley* 458 US 176 in 1982, gave two areas that must be met to determine if a child with a disability is receiving FAPE.

a. Procedural Requirements: Did the district follow the correct procedural requirements and provisions in developing the IEP?

b. Will the districts IEP give the child meaningful educational benefit?

In a more recent court case *N.R. vs. Kingwood Township*, the court decided that the IEP must allow the child "significant learning" and give "meaningful benefit." Previously, I discussed how educators have such low expectations for children with disabilities, and that is why it is important for parents to use the terms "meaningful educational benefit" in trying to make sure that their child receives FAPE.

It is my opinion, after fifteen years as an advocate, that very few children with disabilities actually receive FAPE in the United States. Why? For many reasons:

a. Some school personnel have low expectations for children with disabilities.

b. Some school personnel, limit or refuse to provide educational and related services, that children need. This includes functional skill training, transition plans and services, extended school year services, job training, and assistive technology.

c. In my opinion, special education teachers are sometimes not properly trained, or not supported. I have also met some teachers that are being asked to teach too many children with disabilities at one time, and become overwhelmed.

 d. The curriculums that some school districts use to teach children with disabilities, simply do not work. NCLB now requires that materials used to teach children be **"research based,"** meaning that research has been conducted that ensures that the materials used are effective in teaching children.

e. Children need to be provided, enough appropriate services that will, help them to learn. A lot of schools, limit instruction, to one half to one hour per day per subject. A child with disabilities may require more, especially if they are far behind their grade and age appropriate peers. If an appropriate curriculum is being used, but is not used long enough, or often enough, it may prevent a child from learning.

f. Schools often punish and suspend children for inappropriate behavior that is part of their disability. Very few school personnel do manifestation determination decisions, functional behavioral assessments, and develop positive behavior plans. School personnel also continue to suspend the child with disabilities, for the same behavior, again and again, even though IDEA 2004 does not allow it, if the behavior is part of the child's disability. Schools must start relying on proactive positive interventions, to help increase positive behavior, and decrease negative behavior.

g. Parents are often forced, to pay for IEEs, to prove that their child needs certain special education services. If a parent pays for an IEE, then the education is no longer *"free."*

g. On occasion, parents send their children to private schools that do a better job teaching them, but that costs money.

h.. If parents want reimbursement for the private school tuition, this requires due process. Due process can be expensive; an independent evaluation must be conducted, and some parents may hire a special education attorney.

One of the biggest mistakes that parents make when trying to get FAPE for their child is to use the "B-word." In special education, the "B-word" is "best". . The courts have made it very clear that IDEA does not entitle children to the "best" education; only an "appropriate" education. It is very interesting though that NCLB does appear to set high academic goals for all students. Lots of web sites, are available for information on NCLB. Refer to the end of Chapter 3 which contains a few web addresses.

Lies about Free Appropriate Public Education
1. "Your child can only make three months progress this school year in reading, because of her severe learning disability. Your expectations are way too high!"

In my opinion, children with disabilities are able to learn academics at an average rate, if school districts provide children with appropriate educational and related services, use curriculums that are research based and proven to work, to help children learn. School districts must also provide highly qualified teachers, who are motivated to teach core academic subjects to students with disabilities

I actually hear this one a lot. School personnel would like us to believe, that a lot of parent's expectations are way too high. Even Congress found that low expectations of children with disabilities, is preventing them from learning. I also believe that some children "miss" important academic skills that prevent future academic progress, especially in reading. My son Shaun began attending Sylvan at age seventeen because his reading level (according to tests) was only at a fifth grade level. Most professionals state that a fifth grade reading level is "functionally illiterate." The great employees at Sylvan taught me how important it was to have high expectations for Shaun, and all children, with or without disabilities. They also taught me, how important it was to identify the reading skills, that Shaun "missed" in school; and how to teach him those skills. They found that Shaun had "gaps" in his phonics, and that his vocabulary level was to low. These two things were preventing him from improving his reading level. As soon as they filled in those "gaps" in his phonics, and worked on increasing his vocabulary level, Shaun began bringing up his reading level. Reading was finally fun for Shaun, and he began reading a lot. This helped bring his reading level from fifth grade to twelfth grade in two years. Now, years later my son Shaun reads constantly and is even trying to bring up his academics by trying a few college classes. Thank You, Sylvan!

2. "We cannot give your child more intensive academic services because we are already giving him what we have."

IDEA 2004 states, that all children are entitled to special education and related services, to meet their unique educational needs. Schools must find services that children need, even if they have to pay outside professionals to perform the service. I dealt with this for my own son Shaun. I asked for a self-contained learning disabled class for my son because of his low academic levels, and his severe learning disabilities. My local high school did not have a self-contained learning disabled class, and that is where the dispute began. I have already stated that I was ready to request a due process hearing. The issues were their lack of a self-contained LD class, increased academic services, and unilateral graduation. IDEA 2004 also requires that school districts offer a "continuum of placement options" #300.115(see Easy-To-Understand definitions), which they were not doing. After several meetings, we came to an agreement which helped my son receive an appropriate education. Children with disabilities, must learn to read, do math, spell and do other academics if they have any chance for a happy fulfilled life. Parents should also not forget, that IDEA 2004, also addresses functioning levels and not just academics.

3. "Your child may have Sensory Processing Disorder. But even if she does, we do not think that it affects her education; therefore we do not have to provide any services for it."

Sensory processing disorder, used to be called, sensory integration disorder. Sensory integration means that the senses work together. Sensory integration is an important part of the brains function that is responsible for organizing sensory information for on going use.

If a child has sensory processing disorder they may experience: overly sensitive to touch, movement, sights or sounds, under-reactive to touch, movement sight or sounds, activity level that is high or low, difficulties with coordination, delays in speech and language, delays in fine and/or gross motor skills, difficulties with academics, poor self concept, difficulties with executive functioning, and difficulty with behaviors.

Sensory processing disorder can be part of another disability such as: autism spectrum disorder, ADHD, and learning disabilities. The above difficulties usually negatively affect children's education and lives; and therefore school personnel must provide special education services if a child has this disorder, and requires services. Sensory processing disorder, is often overlooked by parents and school personnel; to the detriment of children with disabilities.

Treatment for sensory processing disorder is sensory integration therapy by a **qualified and trained** occupational therapist (OT). Make sure your schools occupational therapist is trained, before agreeing to have your child receive therapy.

I found a lot of Websites on Sensory Processing disorder. Website **www.autism.healingthresholds.com.** Website **www.sensoryint.com.** Also, there is a book entitled *The Out of Sync Child: Recognizing and Coping with Sensory Processing Disorder, Revised Edition* by Carol Stock Kranowitz and Lucy Jane Miller. This book has a lot of valuable information for parents and school personnel about sensory processing disorder.

4. "Your son's primary label is "behavior disordered." We do not have to give him services for his secondary label of learning disabled."

IDEA 2004 states that school districts must deal with all children's needs, so this is a lie. I have seen an alarming trend in the last several years; of young men with learning disabilities who become teenagers and develop behavioral difficulties. In my opinion the young men, that I have dealt with, have developed behavior problems *because* they are not receiving appropriate educational services for their learning disabilities. When I was in an IEP meeting (advocating for a young man) and was told the above lie, I almost fainted. I turned, looked at the school person who said it, and said "You know that that is not true. Schools must deal with all of the needs of a child with a disability." The school person who said this, then left the room, and never came back. I guess he didn't want to discuss it anymore. Children can and usually will develop negative behavior, if they are not receiving an appropriate education.

Another alarming trend, that I have seen, is the same young men, turning to drugs and alcohol to self medicate. Parents must be careful to be watchful for this trend in their own children. I have seen a few cases of girls doing the same thing, but it seems most prevalent with young men.

5. "We understand that your child's label is emotionally disturbed and needs counseling, but we do not have the staff to provide psychological counseling."

In 2001-2002 when the Office of Special Education Program's (OSEP) came to monitor Illinois's compliance with IDEA, it found that a lot of school districts in Illinois, were not providing psychological counseling and mental health services for children with disabilities. IDEA 2004 requires psychological counseling if a child needs it to benefit from their education. Christopher Koch, EdD from the Illinois State Board of Education issued a memorandum to school districts entitled: "Compliance with State and Federal Regulations Regarding Psychological Counseling and Mental Health Services." The memorandum states: "If restraints of time, training or expertise prevent the use of school personnel for provision of needed psychological and counseling services, it is expected that districts will arrange for outside services to meet individual students needs." Even though this particular memorandum, is written for people in Illinois, the psychological counseling and mental health services are to be given under IDEA 2004 (which is a federal law, and applies to all states). This means all states must give the services. Parents should check with their state board of education, to determine if they have written any memorandums about how school districts are to comply with IDEA 2004, in the areas of psychological counseling and mental health services.

I am including the web site for the US Department of Education. Their website is **www.ed.gov**. Type in special education in the box and you will be transferred to the Office of Special Education and Rehabilitation Services (OSERS). OSEP is the department within OSERS that deals with special education issues. Request a copy of your states last compliance report. Each state is monitored, approximately every seven years, for compliance with IDEA.

School personnel can bill parent's insurance or Medicaid for services, but only **with the parents permission.** Parents should be careful about this, because it may limit the child's ability to get health insurance in the future.

6. "Why don't you just move so that your child can get in that program."

I am always surprised when parents call and tell me that their school district personnel told them to move. I guess they want the parent to move, so that they no longer have to educate the child, or deal with the "assertively persistent" parent!

This does become an issue when only certain school districts have certain programs. In my area one school district, offers the hearing impaired program. Another school district, may have the visually impaired class. I advocated for an eleven year old, young man with autism. It took me several months to find an appropriate placement for him, in another school district. The school agreed to place him in the program, pay for it, and he did very well.

I discourage parents from moving, so that their child can receive FAPE. If parents do not fight for appropriate services, but move instead, nothing is going to change. One mother moved to another part of an affluent suburb in Illinois, so that her child could change school districts and receive FAPE. Things started out pretty well, but within one year, the parent was receiving the same difficulty with the new district than she did with the old district. It was too late though: as she had already sold her first house, and bought a second house.

7. "Your child is seventeen years old and has enough credits, we are graduating him this year."

School personnel, and parents, must take other things into consideration, before they decide to graduate a child, not just whether they have enough credits. Parents as part of the IEP team, need to determine if a child with disabilities needs to be educated past eighteen years of age, to receive FAPE. Things parents need to consider are: Whether the child has made appropriate academic progress in their education, whether the child made progress or completed his or her IEP goals, whether the child is ready for post school learning, and independent living, whether a child has completed all of their transition goals, written on the transition plan, whether the child has received job skill training. Goals should be functional, as well as academic.

Parents also need to consider, that adult services in some states are poor, and the child may not receive an appropriate adult program.

I have included an article, on how parents can use IDEA 2004, to improve their child's special education services. The article, is written by Wayne Steedman, Esq. and is entitled: "Ten Tips: How to Use IDEA. 2004 to Improve Your Child's Special Education #1. This article is used with permission from Wayne Steedman, Esq, and can be downloaded at **www.wrightslaw.com.**

Tip 1. Use the findings and purposes in IDEA. 2004 to establish a higher standard for FAPE. "As the parent or teacher, you need to understand that when Congress reauthorized IDEA 2004, they raised the bar. To meet these new legal requirements in IDEA 2004, schools will have to use research-based instruction and provide more intensive special education services."

2. Use IDEA 2004 and No Child Left Behind to obtain a better IEP. "The purpose of the No Child Left Behind Act is "to ensure that all children have a fair, equal, significant opportunity to obtain a **high quality education** and reach, at a minimum,

proficiency on challenging state academic achievement standards and State academic assessments."

3. Include research-based methodology in the IEP. "By including frequent references to the need to use scientific, research based instruction and interventions, Congress clarified that **methodology is vitally important**. By requiring the child's IEP to include a statement of special education, related services, and supplementary aids and services, based on peer reviewed research. Congress clarified that IEP's must include research based methodology.

4.Ensure that annual goals are comprehensive, specific, and measurable. "Measurable annual goals, including **academic and functional goals.**"

5. Use new evaluation procedures to monitor academic progress and progress on IEP goals. "When conducting an evaluation, the school shall use a variety of assessment tools to gather relevant functional, developmental, and academic information, including information provided by the parents." "To meet the threshold requirements for a FAPE, the school must ensure that the child with a disability makes adequate progress in academic achievement and functional performance, and on the IEP goals. If the child's academic achievement and functional performance are not commensurate with the child's progress on IEP goals, the child's IEP needs to be revised. The parents and educators need to determine what adjustments need to be made to the child's special education program and the IEP."

6. Give consent only for evaluations or portions of the IEP. to which you agree. "If you want to consent to part of the IEP, here are some suggestions:

a. Initial each part of the IEP to which you agree.

b. Next to the signature line, write that you do not consent to any part of the IEP that you did not initial."

7. Insist that the child's regular education teacher participate in IEP meetings. "If you encounter a problem getting the required members of your child's team to attend the IEP meeting, write a letter to request that all of your child's regular education teachers and related service providers attend the IEP meeting."

8. Avoid three year IEPs like the plague. "Find out if your state was approved for the IEP pilot program. If your state was approved for the pilot program, you need to double-check the beginning and ending dates on any IEP for your child."

9. Challenge suspension or expulsion if child's behavior was a manifestation of the disability, or if the alternative placement does not provide FAPE.

"If the school places your child into an alternate setting, you must diligently investigate whether or not the child's IEP is being fully implemented. If the IEP is not being implemented, you may force its implementation through the dispute resolution procedures in the law. One strategy is to challenge the IEP team's determination that the behavior was not a manifestation of the child's disability."

10. Avoid due process hearings if possible. "Due process hearings should be your last resort, after you have attempted all other methods to resolve your dispute. Due process hearings are often expensive, and a lengthy process." "The adversarial nature of due process hearings often creates a wound in the relationship between parents and school personnel that never heals."

Mediation "Parents and schools can attempt to resolve their dispute through mediation. If the dispute is resolved in mediation, IDEA 2004 requires the parties to execute a legally binding agreement that sets forth the terms of the resolution."

Due Process Hearings "If your attempts to resolve your dispute have been unsuccessful, you may decide to request a due process hearing. Consult with an attorney who is knowledgeable about this area of the law first. Many of the pretrial procedures and timelines for due process hearings are new in IDEA 2004. These pretrial procedures are technical and cumbersome."

"You should avoid a due process hearing if possible. The best way to avoid a due process hearing is to prepare for a due process hearing as soon as you realize that you have a disagreement or dispute with the school about your child's special education program. If you have a well organized case and a clear, simple theme, you will be in a stronger position if you need to request a due process hearing."

Chapter 8: Behavior and Discipline

Behavior and Discipline are two of the major areas—in addition to FAPE—where parents and school districts disagree. I have dealt with many situations where school personnel escalate the behavior—which only makes the situation worse--rather than working with the parent and child to decrease the behavior.

There are many Websites that can help parents with their child's behavioral difficulties, including:

1. Website **www.nichcy.org/resources/behavassessasp** . (NICHCY)

2. Website **www.pbis.org**. (the Center on Positive Behavioral Interventions and Support).

3.Website **www.isi.ukans.edu/beachhp.htm.** (the Beach Center on Families and Disabilities).

4. Website **www.circleofinclusion.org** (an organization to support young children).

LIES ABOUT BEHAVIOR/DISCIPLINE

1. "We do not know what is causing your child's bad behavior? Perhaps something at home is causing the behavior?"

Blaming the parent is one tactic that school districts use with parents. I have been blamed many times for my children's behavioral difficulties, as have friends of mine. Parents must stand up to educators who place all the blame on them. I understand that parents are not perfect, and that sometimes things don't always go smoothly at home. But, school personnel frequently blame the parent, without even considering that the school district and personnel, might have contributed to the negative behavior.

When my daughter Angelina was very young and having behavioral difficulties, I began attending conferences and reading books to educate myself about this issue. The first thing that I learned is that children with disabilities, who have behavioral difficulty, are trying to tell us something with their behavior; it is our job to figure out what it is that they are telling us. The second thing I learned is the ABCs of Behavior.

"A" stands for antecedent, which describes what was happening before the behavior occurred, and what prompts the behavior.

"B" stands for the behavior.

"C" stands for the consequence of the behavior.

After the parent and school personnel determine what the ABC's are, they need to figure out specifically what the child is telling them with his behavior. Is the child trying to tell us that the academics are too hard, or are they are tired, or is the child next to them bothering them, or do they need time to calm down as sometimes happens with children with autism. The list could go on and on but these are a few examples. A functional behavioral assessment, which will be discussed later, is used to determine what a child is getting out of the negative behavior.

2. "We are not trained to investigate why your daughter is having behavioral difficulties."

I have had school district personnel tell me this, and my response has been "No problem; you can hire a behavior specialist to figure it out for us." Educators that I have worked with, almost always, back down and try to work with the parent, to figure out what the child is saying by their behavior. Parents should insist that school personnel immediately start tracking the behavior. They should write down the ABCs, the time the behavior occurred, the behavior, the day etc., and send copies to the parent. Parents also need to ask that the school personnel fill out a functional behavioral assessment (FBA) for their child. The person conducting the FBA should have training and experience in the area (Parents need to check, before the FBA is filled out).

Parents should also consider whether there is a physical reason for the negative behavior. When Angelina was in high school her negative behavior got worse when she was tired or not feeling well. The teacher would call me if she thought Angelina was tired, or didn't feel well, and I would bring her home. The next day Angelina would return to school, and do much better.

Some children with autism may have negative behavior when they are overwhelmed, with too many people; or due to sensory processing disorder. If parents and school personnel can determine when and why negative behavior is occurring, they may be able to work together to eliminate or decrease the behavior.

In the NICHCY document "Interventions for Chronic Behavior Problems," it states "Instruction and curriculum need to be adapted to meet the individual needs of the student. When they are not, disruptive behavior can result." Parents need to understand this, and make sure that their child is receiving appropriate academic instruction, to prevent negative behaviors. Parents, must also be sure that their child's IEP is being followed. IDEA 2004 has added a section, that if the child's behavior, is a direct result of the school districts failure to implement the IEP, they must take immediate steps to begin complying with the child's IEP, or modify the IEP as needed.

3. "Alright now, we know why your child is having behavior difficulties, but we don't know what to do about it."

It is my opinion, that most school personnel do understand behavior, and positive behavioral interventions, but they just do not want to take the time to do anything about it, or don't have the personnel to do it.

Once the educators track the behavior, and complete the functional behavioral assessment (FBA), an IEP meeting needs to be scheduled. to address the negative behavior. During the IEP meeting parents need to discuss the tracking of the behavior (time of day, ABCs of behavior, and other details such as does the behavior occur during academic time etc), and the functional behavioral assessment. Portions of a document titled "Functional Behavioral Assessment and Positive Interventions: What Parents Need to Know"#2 are located at the end of this chapter. This article is reprinted, with permission from Pacer Center.

Next, the academic areas need to be discussed, to determine if the child is exhibiting negative behavior to try and avoid academics that are too hard. When my daughter Angelina was in first grade, she would throw herself on the floor every time academics were done. It took a while, but eventually her teacher and I, figured out that she was telling us that the academics were too hard. Once we changed her curriculum to a more functionally based one (daily living skills, cooking, cleaning, community), her behavior became more appropriate. If the child's academics are too difficult, parents need to discuss with educators changes that need to be made, in the academic areas. One thing that can be done, if appropriate, is to include more functional activities in the child's IEP, and fewer academics activities. I am often surprised, by parents of children with disabilities, who only want to focus on academics, and not functional areas; children with disabilities need both.

Some school personnel punish children with disabilities who have negative behavior, rather than figuring out why the child is misbehaving, and how to decrease or stop it. According to the NICHCY document entitled "Interventions for Chronic Behavior Problems, "Punishing, threatening, blaming and criticizing students as a way of influencing their behavior, only works in the short term. What the research shows is that effective teachers tend to rely instead on proactive strategies for preventing behavior problems. They reinforce appropriate behaviors and teach social problem solving." Children with disabilities, may need to be taught, new skills in place of the negative behavior. A plan for teaching these new skills, should be included in your child's IEP.

After all, of this is discussed, a positive behavior plan should be written. (Information on developing a positive behavioral plan is included at the end of this chapter). Parents should also ask for a daily behavior sheet, tracking their child's behavior to be sent home, (and confirm that your request is included in the IEP). If the teacher states she doesn't have time, parents must insist. Read the IEP before you leave, and make sure that a description of your child's negative behavior is in the meeting notes. If it is not, ask that this be included. This way, if the behavior continues--or worsens, the school district cannot state that they did not know about the behavior. Also make sure that the positive behavior plan, is attached to the IEP, and that the teacher understands how to implement it.

5. "IDEA 2004 allows us to punish children with disabilities the same as everyone else."

IDEA 2004 allows schools to discipline children with disabilities the same as children with out disabilities, but only **if the child's behavior is not caused by their disability**. The meeting that is held, to determine if the behavior is part of the child's disability, is called the manifestation determination decision. I believe that the manifestation determination decision, is one of the most important areas that parents must be involved in; to protect their child's rights. Parents must be "assertively persistent" to make sure that their child is not "punished" for behavior that is part of their disability. What IDEA 2004 does not specifically state, but implies, is that *if the behavior is part of the child's disability, they cannot be disciplined, in the same manner, as children without disabilities.*

6. "We can suspend your child for as many days as we want to, and there is nothing you can do about it."

For children with disabilities, IDEA 2004 only allows up to ten days suspension for a violation of student conduct. According to the OSEP position letter dated March 18, 2005; the Supreme Court in Honig v. Doe, 108 S. Ct.592 (1988) "established that a student with a disability could not be unilaterally removed from school for more than ten school days for misconduct that arose from the student's disability." After ten days, school personnel must call a manifestation determination meeting to determine if the behavior is part of the child's disability. If the behavior is part of the child's disability, the IEP team is then required under IDEA 2004 to conduct a functional behavioral assessment (FBA), and implement a positive behavior plan, to prevent the behavior from happening again.

In the OSEP position letter of March 18, 2005 states that "change of placement for disciplinary removals as a removal for more than ten consecutive school days or a series of removals that constitute a pattern because they cumulate to more than 10 school days. . . and because of factors such as the length of each removal, the total amount of time the child is removed, and the proximity of the removals to one another." If a disciplinary change of placement occurs (see above), a manifestation determination decision, must be made. If the behavior is part of the child's disability a functional behavioral analysis (FBA), must be conducted (by a trained person), and a positive behavioral plan must be developed by the child's IEP team.

If the behavior is **Not** due to the child's disability, then they can be disciplined the same as children without disabilities, which means that the suspension could be longer than ten days. IDEA 2004 does require though, that the child continue to receive FAPE. On the eleventh day of suspension, the child should receive educational services that will allow them to continue working on IEP goals.

If school personnel believe that the child's behavior Is **Not** due to their disability, and parents disagree, they may file for a due process hearing. Due process hearings will be discussed in Chapter 9.

7. "We have no choice but to send your son to an interim alternative educational setting (IAES) and we cannot consider your child's unique circumstances."

IDEA 2004 does allow for a removal of a child with disabilities to an interim alternative educational setting (IAES) for 10 school days. This can be done, for a violation of code of student conduct, **but only if this is also done for students without disabilities.**

IDEA 2004 added a section pertaining to the authority of school personnel. This allows school personnel to consider any unique circumstances on a case-by-case basis, when determining if a change of placement should occur. In the past, school personnel have refused to look at each child with a disability individually. Now, school personnel have the authority to consider the child and his or her unique needs, disability, before determining if a change of placement is required.

8. "We are allowed to expel your son because we caught him with a knife."

Children with disabilities cannot be expelled, **unless the behavior is not part of the child's disability;** though some school districts do try and expel children with disabilities. If a parent does not know IDEA 2004 well enough, they may think that school personnel do have the right to expel a child with disabilities, despite the fact that the behavior is a part of the child's disability. I have never met a child with disabilities whose behavior was not a part of their disability, and that is why the manifestation determination decision is a critical one.

School personnel may put a child with disabilities into an interim alternative educational setting (IAES), for not more than forty-five school days; for the following reasons: If the child is in possession of a weapon, knowingly possesses or uses illegal drugs, sells or solicits sale of illegal drugs, or has inflicted serious bodily injury to a person at school. The definition of "serious bodily injury" is a "bodily injury which involves:

a. a substantial risk of death,

b. extreme physical pain,

c. protracted and obvious disfigurement, or

d. a protracted loss or impairment of the function of a bodily member, organ, or mental faculty."

The IEP team, to include the parents, determines what interim alternative educational setting the child goes to. If school personnel want to continue placement at the IAES past forty-five days, and the parents disagree, then the school district must file for a due process hearing. If school personnel do not file for a due process hearing, then the parent may be forced to. The child would stay in the IAES until the due process hearing was completed, and a due process ruling is given.

Parents need to be careful and make sure that any IAES their child is in, continues to provide educational services that their child needs. Many IAES, focus on the negative behavior, and do not provide specialized educational services, that many children with disabilities need.

A few final comments about behavior and discipline.

If a school district continually suspends a child with disabilities, for separate incidents, a parent would have to prove that a "pattern has developed", to prevent the school district from continuing to suspend the child for the same behavior. After a suspension, parents should insist on a functional behavioral analysis, and that a positive behavior plan be developed, to try and decrease or eliminate the behavior.

It is my belief, that school district personnel must stop relying on punishment, to "control" children with disabilities, and start using positive interventions. I have never seen a child with disabilities, not respond to a positive behavior plan. The secret is that the plan, must be properly developed, before a crisis arrives, and must be used consistently.

Some very helpful forms, which can be of assistance to educators and parents, can be downloaded at **www.circleofinclusion.org**. to help educators and parents with behavior. The available forms include a behavioral log, an environmental and curricular checklist, social skill training, a functional behavioral analysis, and behavioral intervention program.

The document "Functional Behavioral Assessment
And Positive Interventions; What Parents Need to Know"#2. Reprinted with permission from PACER Center, Minneapolis **www.pacer.org.**

Positive Behavioral Interventions

Positive: Characterized by or displaying approval, acceptance, or affirmation.

Behavior: What we do.

Intervention: an action that changes a course of events.

Adapted from Merriam Webster's Tenth Collegiate Dictionary.

What is a functional behavioral assessment (FBA)?

FBA is a process for collecting information. The data the team collects, are used to help determine why problem behaviors occur. The data will also help identify ways to address the behaviors. Functional behavioral assessment data are used to develop a positive behavioral intervention plan. The IDEA specifically requires an FBA whenever a child with a disability has his or her current placement changed for disciplinary reasons. This does not mean that we should not think about FBA at other times, too.

Steps in conducting a functional behavioral assessment:

1. Identify and agree on the behaviors that most need to change.

2. Determine where the behaviors occur. and where they do not. Identify what may contribute to the behaviors. The team will ask these kinds of questions:

a. What is unique about the environments where behaviors are not a concern.

b. What is different in the places where the problem behaviors do occur?

c. Could they be related to how the child and teacher get along?

d. Does the number of other students or the work a child is asked to do cause the problem?

e. Could the time of day or a child's mood affect the behaviors?

f. Was there a bus problem or a disagreement in the hallway?

3. Collect data on the child's performance from as many sources as possible.

4. Develop a hypothesis about why problem behaviors occur (the function of the behaviors). A hypothesis is an educated guess, based on data. It helps predict where and why problem behaviors are most likely to occur, and where and why they are least likely to occur.

5. Identify other behaviors that can be taught, that will serve the same function for the child.

6. Test the hypothesis. The team develops and uses positive behavioral interventions. that are written into the child's IEP or behavior intervention plan.

7. Evaluate the success of the interventions. Change or fine tune as needed.

Behavior Intervention Plan

An effective behavior intervention plan (often called a behavior support plan or positive intervention plan) is used to teach or reinforce positive behaviors. Typically, a child's team develops the plan. It usually includes:

a. Skills training to increase appropriate behavior.

b. Changes that will be made in classrooms. or other environments to reduce or eliminate problem behaviors.

c. Strategies to replace problem behaviors with appropriate behaviors that serve the same function for the child.

d. Supports for the child to use the appropriate behaviors.

A POSITIVE INTERVENTION PLAN IS NOT A PLAN TO DETERMINE WHAT HAPPENS TO A STUDENT WHO VIOLATES A RULE OR CODE OF CONDUCT. . .

Examples of behavioral intervention strategies

a. Stop, Relax, and Think teaches children how to think about the problem they are having and find a solution.

b. Planned Ignoring is useful in stopping behaviors that are annoying. Planned Ignoring is not suitable for behaviors that are extremely disruptive.

c. Preventive Cueing lets a child know when he or she is doing something that is not acceptable. Teachers, or parents can frown, shake their head, make eye contact, point to a seat for a wandering child, or snap their fingers, to let the child know he or she needs to pay attention or to stop the problem behaviors.

d. Proximity Control means that a teacher or adult moves closer to the child in a gentle way.

f. Touch Control, meaning touch that is not resisted, is a nonverbal guided intervention. It is used to direct a student toward positive behavior. For example: a teacher may gently place a hand on a child's shoulder to steer the child back to his or her desk.

g. Humor directed either at the teacher or the situation—never at the child—can defuse tensions as well as redirect children.

h. Nonverbal warnings, give a child the opportunity to regain control, without being singled out for a verbal reprimand.

i. Discipline privately. Many children see it as a challenge when teachers attempt to discipline them in front of peers.

j. Positive Phrasing lets children know the positive results for using appropriate behaviors. Teachers and parents are used to focusing on misbehavior.

k.. I messages described by Thomas Gordon in his 1974 book Teacher Effectiveness Training, helps children learn about how their problem behaviors affects others. It also demonstrates the importance of taking responsibility for one's own behavior. For example, parents or teachers will use language like "I'm upset when …? Rather than "You are bad when. . .

l. Behavior Shaping acknowledges that not all children can do everything at one hundred percent.

m. Clear routines and expectations let children know what comes next in their school day, reducing anxiety or fear. Teachers who post and review the rules daily establish expectations for behavior during the day

Children with disabilities, often respond better to a routine that is consistently, carried out every day. Many children will benefit from a daily written schedule. The schedule is gone over with the student every morning (this way if changes occur, the child is made aware of them). The schedule can have pictures if the child is not able to read.

Chapter 9: Due Process and Other Resolution Processes

During my more than fifteen years of advocacy, I have discussed the possibility of parents filing for a due process hearing many times. Usually, the parent's first question is "What is a due process hearing?" After I explain what it is, and what is required to win, most of them run away screaming. I calm them down from their initial panic; and we discuss it rationally.

Parents can win a due process hearing; if they have developed concrete evidence in their child's school record, are properly prepared, and keep the case simple. The first due process hearing that I advocated at; I lost big time. I lost because I did not understand what the process was, and what was necessary to win. I settled the next case (I was up against an attorney), and won the rest. When I was preparing the second case, I spoke to a state board of education employee, about a few questions I had. She stated that I was "crazy" to advocate at a due process hearing "because I was not an attorney." I laughed, because I knew that this was an intimidation tactic. The goal was, I guess, to get me to stop doing due process--which of course I did not do. After I had advocated at several due process hearings, we spoke again, and her attitude seemed to change. The only negative thing she said was, that I didn't charge enough; which I agreed with.

If the case is complicated, or has many issues, parents may need to consult with and consider hiring, a special education attorney or advocate. At the end of this chapter is information on advocates helping parents with due process hearings.

To prepare the case properly due process, requires hundreds of hours of work. This will increase your chances of winning. There are a few things that parents should know about due process:

a. After a parent files for due process, they should have little verbal contact with the school district, unless about a new problem with their child. If a parent must communicate with the school district, do it in writing, short, and to the point. Keep communication, as much as possible, in writing.

b. Once a parent files for due process, some school district personnel become angry and may retaliate against the parent. One parent told me that her school district would not try, and retaliate against her, because she filed for due process. She was quickly surprised when they did, and she apologized, for not believing me. I think parents should expect some type of intimidation or retaliation when they file for due process, not that it is right, but it will more than likely happen. If a parent keeps, most communication with school personnel (after filing for a due process hearing), in writing, this may prevent verbal retaliation against the parent.

c. Once a hearing officer is appointed by the state board of education, he or she cannot have any contact with only one side, without the other side present. This is called ex-parte; and is not allowed. If a phone conference must take place, usually the school district personnel will call the parent, and then the hearing officer; and they will have a three way conversation.

d. Parents must always get an independent educational evaluation (IEE), even if they are only considering filing for a due process hearing. Parents should take their child for the IEE before they file for a due process hearing.

In the third hearing that I advocated at, I insisted that the parent take their child to an independent evaluator. The mother complained about it, stating "I don't have the money, it takes too long etc." I still insisted and she took him. One day, I received a phone call from a woman who was crying very hard. After a few minutes, I figured out that it was the mother from the due process that I was advocating at. I calmed her down, so that I could understand what she was saying. She said "I just received a copy of the report from the independent evaluator. Oh my goodness, you were right, my son has several learning disabilities. This must be why he has always had trouble in school. Why did they not figure out in first through sixth grade that he had a learning disability?" My answer was "Because they do not want to give him special education services." A couple of weeks later, she told me that she was happy, that I insisted on the independent evaluation. The hearing officer ruled that the school district personnel should have known that this young man had learning disabilities, and ruled in the parents favor.

f. Another important thing that parents need to understand about due process, is that some states have a one-tier system, and some states have a two-tier system. Illinois, where I live, has a one-tier system, which means that the hearing officers are appointed and paid by the Illinois State Board of Education. Any appeals go to state or federal court. In a two-tier system, the due process hearing is conducted, by the school district. The losing party must appeal to the state department of education, which appoints a review officer or review panel. After the review officer or panel issues a decision, the losing party can appeal to state or federal court. If you are a parent that is considering due process check with your state board of education and see which tier system your state uses.

In Appendix A there will be a brief summary and time lines; about preparation for a due process hearing. Consider consulting with a special education attorney if you find yourself in a due process hearing; even if you decide to conduct the hearing yourself. The information a special education attorney can share with a parent can be invaluable.

LIES ABOUT DUE PROCESS HEARINGS

1 "If you want to file for a due process hearing you must use a form and send it to the state board of education yourself."

Every state board of education is required to have a due process form available for parents, if they that want to use one; but parents are not required to use it. Actually, I never use a form, I would rather draft the due process request myself. If you are considering due process and are interested in using your states form, contact your state board of education. Parents should make due process requests specific and as short as possible. For Example: Reason 1: Placement. I believe the placement the school is proposing will not give my child FAPE, and will not allow her to make meaningful academic and functional progress. Then list the rest of the reasons.

Don't forget to put what you are proposing as a resolution. Also don't forget reimbursement for independent educational evaluations.

In a one and two-tier state, parents send their due process request to the school district. It is the school's job, within, fifteen days, to send it to the state board of education.

2. "In the due process complaint you can just include what the disagreement is; and figure out what resolution you want later."

This is untrue: The due process complaint must include:

a. the name of the child,

b. the address where the child lives,

c. the name of the child's school

d. a description of the nature of the problem of the child relating to the proposed or refused action, including facts relating to the problem; (Don't go into a lengthy discussion about the disagreement. Just put specific reasons for filing for due process) and

e. A proposed resolution, of the problem to the extent known, and available to you at the time.

A due process complaint must contain all of the above information, to be considered "sufficient" so that the hearing may move forward.

If the school district receives a due process complaint that they do not consider "sufficient," they must notify the other party, and the hearing officer within fifteen days. Within five days of receiving the insufficiency notice, the hearing officer must notify both parties of his or her decision. Sufficiency, doesn't mean whether or not the party filing has a case; just that the due process complaint was filed properly. If the due process request is found "insufficient," the party who filed for due process may re file with all of the correct information.

IDEA 2004 requires that all issues to be heard at the due process hearing must be included in the due process request letter. Changes can only be made if the parent and school personnel agree, **or if a hearing officer agrees.**

If a due process is filed, by either the parent or the school district; the child's placement that he or she is in at the time is called the "stay put" placement. The child stays in the "stay put" placement, until the due process hearing is finished, and the hearing officer issues a ruling. If the parent loses, and files for a state or federal appeal, the child also stays in the "stay put" placement, until the appeal is completed.

3. "If you disagree with the proposed changes to your child's IEP, file for a due process hearing."

Parents should make certain that if school district propose changes to their child's identification, evaluation, placement or any thing else that affects their education; they must receive prior written notice (PWN) from the school district. PWN was discussed, in Chapter 3. There is also a two year statue of limitations on filing for a due process hearing.

Parents need to take into account the new Supreme Court ruling which addresses burden of proof; *Schaffer v. Weast* before they file for due process. The case was about, who had the burden of proof at a due process hearing--the school district--or the parents who filed. The Supreme Court ruled that the person that filed had the burden of proof, except where states already had rules about burden of proof. These states, are not covered by this ruling. Other states will have no change; because the burden continues to be on the party that filed for due process. The rest of the states will have a change, **the burden is now on the party that files for due process.** If you are not sure how your state rules on burden of proof at due process contact your state board of education. In Illinois where I live, there is a law that states that the burden of proof at a due process hearing, belongs to the school district.

Schaffer vs. Weast does have a positive benefit though. This Supreme Court ruling, clarifies that school districts have an **obligation** to file for a due process hearing; if the parent does not consent to the proposed changes to the child's IEP. In the past, many parents were forced, to file for a due process hearing, because school districts refused to. This represents a great change for parents; since burden of proof may be on the party that files (depending on where you live). This may work to parents advantage to have school districts file the due process request.

4. "We know you are still waiting to begin the due process procedure but we have not heard from the state board of education yet; and it may take months."

Once the school district receives a request for a due process hearing, they are required under IDEA 2004 (in a one-tier state), to notify the state board of education within five days. They should also send a copy of the evidence of delivery of the due process request; by certified mail, to the parent.

Within five days, from the time the state board of education receives the request for due process, they must appoint a hearing officer (in a one-tier state). Due process has very specific timelines that must be adhered to, unless both parties agree to the exceptions.

5. "IDEA 2004 does not allow us to give your child compensatory services; even if you file for a due process hearing."

Actually compensatory services are allowed under IDEA 2004; but they are very hard to get, without a due process hearing. Compensatory services are future educational services given to a child with disabilities; to make up for the school districts failure to provide FAPE. Parents should ask for compensatory services as an issue; in a due process hearing. In the Federal Court case *Kevin T. vs. Elmhurst Community School District #205.* The court gave *Kevin T.* compensatory services until the age of 22; because the district denied him FAPE.

6. "We know the hearing officer used to work for this district, but we believe that he can be unbiased, and still want him to hear the case."

IDEA 2004 does not allow a hearing officer to hear a due process case if:

a. the individual ever worked for the district, or special education cooperative,

b. the individual resides in the district, or

c. if the appointee has an apparent personal, professional, or financial interest that would interfere with his or her objectivity, regarding the matter at issue.

The one major problem, I see with the due process system, is that some times the hearing officers are biased, against the parent and child. Some of the hearing officers, may have had a previous relationship with school personnel. The most important thing in a due process case is who the hearing officer is, and if he or she can render a fair and impartial due process ruling. The entire premise of due process is that it is to be a fair and impartial system, to resolve special education disputes.

7. "I know that we are supposed to have a resolution session, but you don't have to attend."

Resolution sessions are brand new in IDEA 2004. The resolution session is mandatory for parents. School district personnel, and parents, may agree to "waive" (not have) the resolution session, but make sure it is in writing, and signed by both parties. If parents do not attend the resolution session, the school district may ask, that the due process complaint, be dropped by the hearing officer. The purpose of the resolution session, is to see if a settlement, can be reached, between school district personnel and parents. If the parent does not bring an attorney to the resolution session, then the school district, may not bring an attorney. I haven't read anything though, that does not allow the parent to bring an *educational advocate* to the resolution session, and they should if possible. Within fifteen days of receiving the due process complaint, the school district must hold the resolution session. I have spoken to several parents, who have attended resolution sessions with their school districts. Their opinion is, that some school districts are not using the resolution session, to try and settle the case, but to try and figure out what the parents case is. Parents should bring no evidence to the resolution meeting, except a list of resolutions that they are willing to accept. IDEA 2004 states that parents attendance is mandatory, it does not state that they have to reveal what their case is to the school district.

I found a good free document on resolution sessions: *Resolution Meetings: A Guide for Parents* on the Website **www.taalliance.org**.

8. "Alright, we will agree to give you what you want, but we are not going to write it down. You will just have to trust us."

Verbal agreements, are not worth the paper they are written on. All agreements of any kind, between parents and school personnel, must be in writing; mediation due process etc. IDEA 2004 has added legally binding written settlement agreements. This is an important development for parents, who had written agreements with school districts in the past, and the school personnel refused to comply with them. Now with the changes that IDEA 2004 brings, if a school district writes down a settlement, it is legally binding. If the school refuses to comply with the written settlement agreement, the parent can now go to state or federal court and ask a judge to compel the school district to comply. IDEA 2004 does allow though, that either party may void the legally binding written agreement within three business days.

9. "The due process hearing must be held at our administrative offices."

The due process hearing, must be held at a mutually convenient time and place, for parents and school personnel. What this means, is that the due process hearing, does not have to be held on school property. In Illinois, the place that the due process hearing is held may not be rented by either party. I knew a parent that was able to use her town's hall to have the due process hearing. Check with your state board of education, about your states rules, about places where a due process can be held.

10. "We know that you won your due process hearing but that does not mean that we automatically have to pay for your attorney fees."

Actually this is partially correct, its not automatic, a parent must go to state or federal court in order to recover attorney fees for winning a due process case. Attorney fees must be reasonable "and based on rates prevailing in the community in which the action or hearing arose. . ." This was taken from the OSEPs Model Form on procedural safeguards.

Sometimes there is a dispute, between parents and school personnel, over who actually won the due process hearing. This issue could be taken, to federal or state court, at the same time as reimbursement for attorney fees.

11. "Since you lost the due process hearing; you will have to pay our attorney fees as well as your own."

IDEA 2004 has added a provision that states that a court may award reasonable attorney fees to a school district for the following two reasons:

a. a parents attorney filed a complaint or court case that the court finds is **frivolous, unreasonable, or without foundation,** or

b. continued to litigate after the litigation clearly became **frivolous, unreasonable, or without foundation.**

A court can also award reasonable attorney fees to a school district, if your request for a due process hearing or later court case, was presented for any improper purpose such as to harass etc.

Actually, I was told by a special education attorney, that this rule already existed in other laws (Rule of Civil Procedure Rule 11), but that it is newly included in IDEA 2004.

Parents should not be frightened into not filing for a due process hearing; because they are fearful of having to pay the school's attorney fees. I believe that school personnel will use this rule, to intimidate parents into not filing for due process. There is an article on Wrightslaw entitled *New School District Attorneys' Fees Provision under IDEA 2004* by Jess Butler, Esquire. It is a good article on the subject, and parents should go to Wrightslaw, and read it.

As a parent, you are your child's only advocate, and must not let them down; by refusing to fight for a free appropriate public education.

12. "If you want to file for an appeal of the due process decision, you must hire an attorney."

On May 21, 2007 the Supreme Court ruled on the case *Winkelman vs. Parma;* which was about, whether parents had the right to represent their child's interests, under IDEA 2004, in court, without an attorney. The Supreme Court ruled that parents have to right to proceed *pro se* (without an attorney) in all IDEA cases. This is a major victory for parents, who often cannot afford a special education attorney to appeal a due process ruling.

I hope that this Supreme Court ruling, will somewhat level the playing field between parents and school districts.

LAST THOUGHTS ABOUT DUE PROCESS

One of the most difficult parts of due process for me, was dealing with the motions of school district attorneys. I still remember the first time I received a motion for summary judgment; I was scared and didn't know what to do. Summary judgment is a motion that is usually filed with the hearing officer, by the non complaining party (usually the school district), stating that the complaining party does not have a good enough case to go to due process. It is then the job of the hearing officer to make a ruling. In Illinois hearing officers, to my knowledge, are only giving school districts summary judgment if the parent does not show up for the hearing. Though since the changes brought about by IDEA 2004, hearing officers may start giving summary judgment if parents do not attend the resolution session. If a parent or advocate receives a motion, of any kind, from the schools attorney, they must respond within approximately ten days. Parents can get on Wrights law Website at **www.wrightslaw.com** and look for case law, that applies to their case. An advocate can just do the best they can do. I won that motion for summary judgment, by the way; and the case went to a due process hearing; which I also won.

Due process is an extremely adversarial process. When a parent contacts me and states that they will be filing for a due process hearing; I ask them to give me a little time, to see if I can help resolve the issues. Sometimes I am able to, and sometimes the school has dug their heels in, and refuses to even consider a settlement. This extra time though, gives parents the time to get an IEE. Parents should also consider hiring an advocate, or consulting with a special education attorney. This person should have experience with your school district, and also an understanding of due process hearings. Unfortunately, not all advocates do. Parents must not consult with an attorney, who does not practice special education law; because they may not understand the intricacies of this specialized area.

Advocates conducting due process hearings

In some states, advocates are not legally allowed, to conduct due process hearings. The courts in Delaware, ruled that an advocate cannot help a parent with a due process hearing; while the courts in Florida ruled that advocates can help a parent with a due process hearing. As part of this debate, some school personnel are now accusing advocates of "Practicing law without a license." As far as I know, no advocates have successfully been prosecuted for this. If you are an advocate that helps parents with due process hearings, check your states court rulings, to make sure that you can legally advocate at due process hearings.

Each time I conducted a due process hearing, I asked that the hearing officer allow me to go first. Even though in my state, the burden of proof is on the school district. I did this because I could put *my* evidence in front of the hearing officer first, which I believe allows the hearing officer the chance to see what the parents feel the true issues are in the case. If the school district goes first, then the parent must rebut their case as well as put on their own case. In my first due process, the school went first, and were able to get issues heard that had nothing to do with the case; this just muddied the waters.

I would like to make a few comments about the cost of due process for parents. I tried to conduct most of the hearings that I advocated for, on a shoestring budget and did pretty well. If the parents or advocate do not have a printer, printing costs will be quite high. Even with a printer, I could not make the amount of copies at home of all of the needed documents for due process. I saved money by putting the documents in the printer, at the office supply store, myself. This takes a lot of time, but does save money. Parents must also pay for the time that the independent evaluator testifies. I also went through a lot of paper, pencils, and post-it notes also. All letters and documents mailed, must be mailed certified with a return receipt requested; so that you have proof that you sent it. This can be very costly. I do believe though that sometimes parents must spend the money, so that their children can receive FAPE The cost of due process is one of the major reasons that I believe few children in America actually receive a free appropriate public education!

Chapter 10: Frequently Asked Questions and Mistakes Parents Make

I will be starting this chapter with frequently asked questions, and end the chapter with mistakes parents make.

1. "Aren't you afraid that the school district personnel will retaliate against your child, for standing up to them?"

My children are now adults, but when they were children my answer was always the same: "Absolutely not." I have always randomly visited my children's classes to make sure that everything was going well. Over the years, I have found a few issues; but I was there to make sure that my children were receiving an appropriate education. I also believe that parents can develop a good relationship with the teacher, by checking in occasionally. Another benefit, is that if a problem develops, the parent will be aware of it before the situation gets too problematic?

2. "Who is responsible for enforcing IDEA 2004?"

My answer is always the same: "Legally the state board of education is responsible for making sure that school district's obey IDEA 2004. The federal government is responsible for making sure that states obey IDEA 2004." But, the reality is that parents are the enforcement mechanism of IDEA 2004. The federal government only monitor's each state approximately every seven to eight years. The states only monitor the school districts every several years also; unless a certain school district receives a lot of complaints. I was involved with a school district that was monitored by the Illinois state board of education because of many complaints, and due process requests filed. My state calls this a compliance review. Even if the federal or state government find's violations of IDEA; they will probably not be fixed. I have been involved with school districts that have been monitored for compliance with IDEA, and few of the areas were ever fixed. I mentioned previously, that I was on the OSEP advisory board when they came to monitor Illinois's compliance with IDEA. I agreed with all of the areas of non-compliance that OSEP found. What I disagreed with, was what Illinois did to fix the non-compliance. In some cases, all Illinois did, was send letters to school districts; clarifying what IDEA required (which was the law in affect at the time).

3. "Does IDEA 2004 allow parents of children with disabilities to pick their child's teacher?"

IDEA 2004 is silent on this issue. I usually investigated what teachers were available for my son, for the next school year, and discussed the options with my son's current teacher. I always asked that the teacher decision be made before the annual IEP meeting, so that the new teacher could be present. My school district was willing to allow me to be involved in the decision. Things were different for Angelina; because she usually had the same teacher for several years. Parents should ask to be involved in selecting a new teacher for their child--and hope fully the school personnel will agree.

4. "How can a parent pick a "good" advocate to help them advocate for an appropriate education for their child?"

This question came from a good friend of mine, who has had several advocates, help her with her children's education. She has assured me, though that I am her favorite! I think that there are several characteristics, of a good advocate, that a parent can look for:

a. A good advocate, must know the education laws, that they need to help children with disabilities. I have been amazed by people who call themselves "advocates," but don't know IDEA 2004 or NCLB. A good advocate, does not have to memorize the law, but should be able to find something in the law, if they need it. Very few advocates in my area (that I am aware of), are using No Child Left Behind to help children learn academics. A good advocate should use any law, or even case law, that supports their case.

b. A good advocate should not make false promises to parents. One of the very first things, that I tell parents, is that there are no guarantees of the outcome of my advocacy. I always try my best, but unfortunately, I do lose occasionally. Thank fully, I have been pretty successful, but an advocate cannot guarantee that they will be successful. If a parent is using an advocate, and the advocate *promises* success, then I would be concerned about using this person.

c. A good advocate should be passionate about your child, and the educational services that your child needs. If an advocate is not passionate about your child, they may not be willing to help you for the length of time that it takes to get your child an appropriate education. I have been involved with some families for months, to help ensure that their child receives FAPE. No body ever said special education advocacy was easy or quick!

d. A good advocate should not be afraid to stand up to school personnel, when they disagree with them. I have dealt with advocates in the past, that were not willing to speak up at an IEP meeting, even if they disagreed with educators. A good advocate must work for the child first and the parent second. If the advocate is afraid to say anything, they are not going to be successful in getting the child a free appropriate public education.

e. A good advocate should never give away a confidence of the parent, or tell the school, what the parent's advocacy strategy is.

f. A good advocate brings up at an IEP meeting, any educational law that supports their case. Parents are not always familiar with IDEA 2004 and NCLB, and depend on the advocate to assist them in this area.

g. A good advocate never brings up their own child's problems at an IEP meeting. I have mentioned my children in IEP meetings, but usually related to an educational service that helped them, not a problem.

h. A good advocate dresses and acts professionally. I always wear dress pants and a nice top, and always try to act professionally

i. A good advocate tries to understand the parent's needs, as well as the child. Many parents have disabilities themselves that may need to modifications, so that they can participate in the IEP process. I have worked with a couple of parents who had a disability themselves, and I tried very hard to make sure that the school district made modifications when needed.

j. A good advocate is detail oriented, and makes sure that every service promised is in writing. The advocate should check the IEP document, and make sure that the service is written, in a correct manner, so that the parent and the IEP team understand how the service is to be given.

5. "Is the school district allowed to shorten my child's school day, due to transportation?"

No! The law states that every child with a disability has the right to full educational opportunity (which I interpret to mean a full school day). I do not understand why educators don't think it is important for children with disabilities to be in school, the same amount of time as children without disabilities. I have always wanted to ask school personnel why they do not take children with out disabilities out of school early for transportation. But, I already know the answer: The parents of the children without disabilities would be outraged! Where is our outrage? Why are so many parents apathetic about unfair and discriminatory treatment? Unfortunately, I do not have an answer for this one. But, one thing I do know, a lot of anger that parents of children with disabilities have is justified. Parents just need to learn appropriate ways of dealing with their anger.

6. "Is it ever okay to get upset at an IEP meeting?"

Yes it is. But, if you find yourself screaming, yelling, and cussing, the anger has gone too far. Here is an Example: I was in an IEP meeting with a friend of mine several years ago, for her son with autism. The school district personnel had treated her son quite badly for several years. The school district finally was going to allow her son to attend the regular public school, and we were meeting to set up his special education program. At one point, the special education coordinator became upset, and stated that certain behaviors would not be accepted in the school. The mother looked at me, raised her voice slightly, and told the school personnel how upset she was at they way they had treated her son. It was obvious that the mother was upset, but she did not scream or use curse words. The meeting ended shortly thereafter. On the way out, the mother apologized to me for getting upset. I asked her, "Did I stop you?" She said, "No, why didn't you?" My answer was simple: "Because they deserved it." Sometimes, a little righteous indignation can really work! Just tone it down a little bit.

When I advocate for a parent that is extremely angry (justified or not), I ask them, whether they want to be angry or whether they want to work to get appropriate services for their child. I have always had the parent say, that they would rather see that their child receives, appropriate educational services. I tell the parents that we can discuss the anger and frustration amongst ourselves, but when we are with school personnel, we will act professionally. Anger sometimes, must be put aside, for the good of the child.

7. "Why do some school personnel not want to admit that a child has autism; even if it is obvious to everyone?"

I do not consider myself any kind of an expert on autism; but I have advocated for several children who the school district refused to diagnose with autism; even though it was obvious to me, and in my opinion was obvious to them too. For one child, I practically had to beg. The only reason that I convinced them, is because they had already given the child an autism rating scale, which showed that he was likely to have autism. They finally agreed and added autism to the child's label.

Why do some school personnel not want to label children with autism? I believe there are several reasons:

a. Children with autism usually require quite a few special education and related services. School personnel in some cases, do not want to pay for the special education and related services that most children with autism require.

b. School personnel sometimes say that an autism diagnoses is medical, but school psychologists can give a child an autism label, if they wanted to.

c. In my experience, school district personnel often want parents to bear the expense of diagnosing a child with autism, and parents should fight against this.

If a parent suspects that their child has autism, they should immediately write a letter to the person in charge of special education in their school district. This letter should be dated and state why you think that your child has autism. Also, add that you are requesting a Childhood Autism Rating Scale, or a CARS (available on Pro Ed's Website **www.proedinc.com**) be conducted on your child. There are many autism rating scales; but in my opinion the CARS is the best one for children. The CARS also has a section, which tells parents and educators, whether the child has mild, moderate, or severe autism. Parents need to make sure that the school is not offering a GARS which is the Gilliam Autism Rating Scale; which is used for older children and adults

d.. Some children with Pervasive Developmental Disorder (PDD), do not fit into the schools tight definition of "autism."

8. "Why doesn't my local district just give my child the service that they need?"

Special education coordinators (which is what most districts call the person in charge of special education), are often called "gatekeepers." In other words, if a parent thinks that their child needs special education or related services they must get by the "gatekeeper". This is the way I explain this to parents: If their are ten children in front of me, each needing speech therapy, how many of the children's parents are going to fight for the needed service? In my opinion, probably two or three. That means that the "gatekeeper" has been successful in not having to provide or pay for speech therapy for the rest of the seven to eight children.

9. "What is the worst school meeting that you ever went to? And, how would you handle it differently?

The absolute worse meeting that I ever attended, was led by the school districts attorney, who refused to allow the mother (a friend of mine) to say anything. Every time the mother, or I spoke up, we were told to be quiet. I took lots of notes, and was so frustrated. After the meeting, my friend began considering due process; but the school district settled with her, before she had the chance to file.

If this occurred today, I would tell the mother to cancel the meeting; and file a complaint with the Illinois State Board of Education. The complaint would state, that the school having their attorney at an IEP meeting, would prevent her, the parent from being an equal participant.

During the period that I was having a dispute with my high school district, the coordinator stated that their attorney would be coming to one of my son's IEP meetings. I stated "Really? Then I am not coming. I am in the middle of a divorce, and cannot afford to bring my own attorney". The coordinator then said "I guess we won't have him come." I said "Not if you want me to come." If he would have insisted, I would have filed a complaint, with my state board of education. While IDEA 2004 doesn't say, that schools can't bring attorneys to IEP meetings; it discourages it. I would have told the state board of education that the school would have an unfair advantage; because they had an attorney and I didn't.

MISTAKES PARENTS MAKE

1. Letting emotions get the best of you.

The biggest mistake that I believe parents make, in trying to get an appropriate education for their child, is letting their emotions get in the way. I remember one IEP very vividly. I was sitting in the meeting, helping a mother, who was trying to get educational services for her daughter. All of a sudden, she began screaming so loudly that it startled me, and I almost fell off my chair. The school personnel tried hard not to laugh. They reminded me of that time, quite often. Normally I can tell when a parent is getting upset, and I usually take a break, but she surprised me. If a parent is in a meeting and feels themselves getting upset, they should ask for a break.

2. Forgetting your inner voice.

The second biggest mistake that parents make is that they give too much weight to what school personnel say, rather than trusting their own instincts. Parents have told me that they have difficulty standing up to educators, because their parents taught them to "respect" authority. My parents taught me to "respect" authority also, but that doesn't mean I should allow school personnel to get away with lies. If parents don't stand up to educators lies, then their child probably will not receive an appropriate education. Several years ago, when my children were young, the special education coordinator in my elementary school district had resigned. I stopped by her office with a small present, and she told me that she wanted to talk to me. She closed the doors of her office, and closed the screen, which surprised me. We sat down and this is what she said to me, "JoAnn I never understood, until I had children, why you fight so hard for yours; but I understand now! Never stop fighting for your children, because no one else will!." I was shocked! I never expected her to say that, and I have never forgotten it! This applies to all parents, not just me. We must be "assertively persistent" so that our children can receive an appropriate education.

3. Accepting lies from school personnel.

The third mistake parents make is not standing up to the lies of educators. Parents do not necessarily have to stand up to the lies in person. Writing a letter to the person, stating what they said, gives you concrete evidence if you ever need it. I still hope that by making educators accountable, the lies may stop. One time during my divorce, I asked a friend of mine to accompany me to an IEP meeting, which she did. During a break in the meeting, she turned to me, and said, "The school personnel know, that you know the law, better than they do. If they treated you that badly, then there is absolutely no hope for the rest of us parents." I understand her frustration but I do believe that parents can be successful advocates for their child; if they are "assertively persistent".

Conclusion

I would like to conclude this book by sharing with you what a parent from COPAA recently posted on the listserv. The parents name is Marcie Lipsitt, from Michigan, and she has given me permission, to include this in my book. "I go back to a concern raised by a leading national advocate for students with disabilities who said many months ago; "my greatest concern is the lack of outrage and outcry from parents."

"Until every parent of a student with a disability; every parent advocate, every special education attorney. . .understands that we **are in a war for our children's educational lives;** this situation will not even remain status quo, it will deteriorate."

This book has given you the ammunition you need to advocate for an appropriate education for your child. Be vigilant, even if things seem to be going well! The rest is up to you .Good Luck! Remember, your child is depending on you!

Below is a poem I wrote several years ago, hope it inspires you to keep dreaming!
Dreams

When my daughter Angelina was born, I had many dreams, my dreams for her were filled with success.
Doctor, lawyer, it was anyone's guess.

One day, I got the word that my dreams were not to be.
They lay at my feet like a shattered, dead tree.

I realized that if I were to survive, I had to find new dreams—new hopes for our new lives.

Time went on and new dreams were born
Even though sometimes, I stop and mourn

I mourn for the world, who may not see;
what a terrific person that Angelina can be.

I mourn for Angelina, who is often misunderstood,
and I pray for the day when she will be accepted and understood.

I mourn for the people, who would benefit,
From her compassion and generosity of spirit.

My new dreams for Angelina will allow her to be free, To develop into a beautiful blossoming tree.

You see, dreams never die, no matter how hard things get. We change them along the way, so everyone's needs are met.

Please don't stop dreaming because life gets tough.
Change them and mold them, and even if they're rough.

We'll smooth them out along the way and our dreams will continue, Come what may!

Appendix A: A brief summary of How to Prepare for a Due Process Hearing

This information is meant, only as a brief summary, and should not be taken as the only preparation needed for due process. Parents should seek legal advice from a special education attorney, about due process, if at all possible.

Childs history for the due process request

Savannah Johnson is seventeen years old, and was diagnosed with learning disabilities, when she was seven years old. Her learning disabilities are in the areas of written expression and reading; she also has a visual processing disorder. Savannah has been receiving special education services for nine years. At seven years of age, Savannahs full scale IQ was 112, at ten years of age her full scale IQ was 92, at thirteen years of age her full scale IQ was 85, and at her recent reevaluation her full scale IQ was 79. Her current academic levels of functioning are as follows: reading fourth grade, written expression fifth grade, according to the school districts latest testing. Savannahs grades are poor, and the recent academic testing (by the school district), showed that Savannah is making little to no academic progress. There is no transition plan, vocational training, functional skills, or independent living skills training. In fact, school personnel have refused, to even test Savannahs independent living skills. The school has notified Savannah's mother that they are graduating her next year, when she is eighteen years old. Savannahs mother asked for an IEE at public expense, because she disagrees with their recent evaluation, and was verbally denied by school personnel. Savannah's mother also thinks that she may have some undiagnosed disabilities. The school district is also refusing to offer any remediation for Savannah's visual processing disorder, or low academic levels.

Example of a due process request letter

Name of school superintendent

School district name

Address

City, State, and Zip

Date

Dear

This letter, is to formally request, a due process hearing for my daughter Savannah Johnson. Her birth date is XX and she attends Name of School. The issues are as follows:

1. Savannah needs an independent educational evaluation at public expense with a Clinical Psychologist because her reported full scale IQ (according to school testing) has dropped from 112 at seven years of age, to 75 (borderline mental retardation) this year at seventeen years of age. The psychologist needs to determine if in fact her full scale IQ has dropped, and the reason why. Savannah also needs educational testing to determine what her academic levels are; and to determine what remediation she needs for her visual processing disorder; and low academic levels.

2. Savannah is not receiving appropriate special education services or an appropriate placement to meet her educational needs.

3. Savannah deserves compensatory services to make up for lack of FAPE for the last two years. (There is a two year, statue of limitation on due process requests).

4. Savannah has had no transition plan. This plan should include transition services, vocational training, functional skills, and independent living skills if required

5. The school district has refused to test Savannahs functional skills and independent living skills, to see if she needs individualized training in this area.

6. Savannah requires education beyond 18 years of age due to her low academics, her learning disabilities, her lack of transition planning, vocational training, and possible need for functional skills and independent living skills training.

Proposed Resolution

1. 2. and 5. The school district will provide an independent evaluation at public expense with a Clinical Psychologist, of the parents choosing, for the following reasons:

a. To determine if Savannahs full scale IQ has dropped from 112 to 75 over the last several years, as the school district states. If it has dropped, the psychologist can determine why. I am asking for a cost and geographic waiver, due to the severity of my daughters disability, IQ dropping, and lack of local independent evaluators.

b. To determine what appropriate educational program and placement Savannah needs, in order to make progress in her education. Also, what academic special education services for reading and writing she needs, and remediation for her visual processing disorder.

c. To test her independent living skills, using the Scale of Independent Behavior. The psychologist can use the results to determine how much independent living skills training Savannah needs, or if she needs any. Also any additional testing needed for her functional skills.

d. To test all of her academic levels.

e. To determine if Savannah has any undiagnosed disabilities.

3. Compensatory services in the form of tutoring, with an outside private business, (possibly Sylvan). This should be for two hours a week, or eight hours a month for 12 months; which is a total of 96 hours.

4. The school district will write a transition plan to include vocational training, any transition services that Savannah needs, functional and independent living skills (determined by Scale of Independent Behavior).

6. The school district will educate Savannah through the age of 21 years (until she reaches the age of 22).

I will expect to hear from you within 10 days to set up the resolution session. I will not be bringing an attorney to the resolution session, so I understand that the school district cannot have one also. I will see you at the resolution session.

Linda Johnson

Address

City, State and Zip

Hand deliver a copy of the due process request, to the school superintendent's office, and keep a copy.

Before you file for a due process request:

1. Parents should call the school and request to review their child's entire school record (temporary, permanent, E mails or internal memos). Copy any thing specific that will help your case. Next parents should write a letter and request a complete copy of their child's temporary, and permanent, school record. In the request, ask for any internal memos or E Mails related to your child. The reason to review the records before asking for a copy, is because then you will know what is in your child's school record, and you can make sure the entire record is sent to you.

Schools may charge a reasonable fee, but must also have policies in place for parents to receive free copies of school records if they are unable to pay for them. Take the records and make sure the oldest records are on the bottom and the newer records are on the top. Once they are in the proper order, take a pencil, and number them in the right bottom corner. Start with the newest document; the first page would be #1, the second page #2 etc, continued until all pages are numbered. This is important because later they may get mixed up; and you will need to know how to put them back in order. The first couple of due process hearings I advocated, at I did not do this, and I was unable to put them back in order--oh what a mess.

Once the records are in order and numbered, start going through them for concrete evidence that you can use to prove your case. Mark the pages, of the record you can use, with a brightly colored Post-It note. Use a pencil to mark the information on the document that you want to use (the pencil marks can be erased later).

Check older IQ scores, to see if there is a large drop in your child's IQ score. As stated previously, it is well known in the disability field that a child's IQ will only drop for two reasons--a traumatic brain injury, or an inappropriate education. Check state-district-wide testing to determine if your child has made educational progress.

2. Parents must know what the issues are before they file for a due process hearing. IDEA 2004 states that a due process complaint can only be amended, if both sides or the hearing officer agree. To determine what the issues are, parents should take their child for an independent evaluation. Make sure the evaluator you choose is willing to write a report specifically stating what services your child needs; and has the proper credentials. If the evaluator is a medical professional, make certain that the report is written, using educational terms, not medical terms. The report may take two weeks to one month from the date of the evaluation. When you receive the evaluation report, read it several times, and see if the evaluator wrote something that you may disagree with, or if something is written that you do not want revealed. If there is, contact the evaluator and ask if he or she would consider changing the report. It is ultimately up to the evaluator, if they will change the report.

The independent evaluator may need to testify at the due process hearing if there is one. Parents may need to pay the evaluator for their time and testimony, but you can deal with that later.

Once a parent receives the IEE report, they must decide whether to take the report to the school district, or immediately file for a due process hearing. If a parent brings the IEE report to the school district and they refuse to use the recommendations; the parent can then file for a due process hearing. Or, the parent can immediately file for a due process hearing, and use the IEE report as evidence.

3. The due process complaint must include the following information:

a. The name of the child

b. The address of the child

c. The name of the child's school

d. A description of the nature of the disagreement, and

e. A proposed resolution to the disagreement.

Keep the nature of the disagreement brief, and number them if there is more than one area of disagreement. For Example: If the issue is placement; then state:

#1 Placement. The Placement the school district is offering is not appropriate for my child; because it will not allow for enough remediation for academics that my child needs.

Resolution. The resolution for this would be placement in a self- contained learning disability class for all academics, and regular education placement for crafts, special projects, recess, etc.

Include every issue brought up by the Independent Evaluator. Try to limit the issues to three or four. Remember to ask for reimbursement of the independent evaluation as an issue. I recommend not filing on FAPE as much as you can, unless you have a lot of evidence. For example: If your child's IQ has dropped fifty points, then I would say "My child's lack of educational progress and decrease in IQ shows that he has not received FAPE." Otherwise, be very specific about what the issue is. If the parent believes that the stay put placement is going to be an issue; then they should add that to the due process request letter. For Example: "I am invoking the stay put provision of IDEA 2004 so that my child can stay in her current placement until the due process hearing decision is given, or the disagreement, is resolved in writing." Hand deliver the due process request to your school superintendent's office, and of course keep a copy.

4. Within five days (in a one tier state), your state board of education will assign a hearing officer, and will notify both sides.

5. You should hear from school district personnel within ten days to schedule the resolution session. The session should be at a convenient time and place for parents and school personnel. Have an advocate or friend go with you, don't go alone. Bring no evidence, but bring paper to take notes; and also a list of resolutions that you would be willing to accept. Parents should listen to what school personnel have to say, and talk very little. School personnel may ask questions, to try and figure out,

what your case will be at due process; make your answers short. If an agreement is reached, make sure it is in writing, is signed by the parent and school personnel, and that you are given a copy. Either side may void the written settlement agreement within three days. The school district has a total of thirty days to resolve the issues in the due process complaint.

6. If parents, have not been given PWN, they should receive this in writing within ten days.

7. If the school district thinks that the due process claim is not sufficient, they must let the hearing officer know, in writing, within fifteen days. Parents should not be worried about this, but should respond in writing to the districts sufficiency claim.

8. Within ten calendar days of receiving the due process complaint, the non-complaining party (the party who did not file for due process) must send a written response to the complaining party that addresses the issues in the due process complaint. For example: If parents file for a due process hearing with five issues, the school district must send the parent, within ten calendar days, a written response to the five issues.

9. During the thirty-day resolution period, parents should use the time to prepare for the due process. Research any due process hearings conducted by your hearing officer, on your state board of education's web site. Parents also must prepare for the first conversation between themselves, the school districts representative, and the hearing officer. Also, take any test scores that you want to use at due process, and make graphs of them. Keep a copy of the test scores close to the graphs, so that you can prove at due process that the scores on the graph are the same scores from your child's testing.

10. After, the thirty-day resolution period, the hearing officer will contact you about scheduling a phone conference between yourself, the school district and the hearing officer. The hearing officer, is not allowed to only talk to one party, without the other party present: That is called *ex parte*. Usually the school district, calls the

hearing officer, and then they call the parent. Many things will be discussed, during this first three-way phone call, which could include such topics as:

a. The dates, and times of the pre-hearing conference (which is usually done by telephone).

b. Parents need to ask for copies of due process forms to include witness lists, document lists, subpoena's for witnesses.

c. Date, time, and location of the due process hearing. The hearing does not have to be held at the school district. Check with your state board of education about rules of due process location.

d. Which side presents their case first. (Parents should ask to go first).

e. Parents should request sequestration of witnesses (this means that all witnesses may not talk to other witnesses and cannot listen to other witnesses testify).

f. The order that the witnesses are going to testify.

g. Any motions that the school wants to bring. The motions that I have seen are a motion for summary judgment, (summary judgment is a motion that one party makes, which means that the other party has no case; and the due process should be dismissed), a motion to exclude witnesses, and a motion to exclude evidence. The parent or advocate must answer these motions in writing (in other words, why the hearing officer should not grant the schools motions). The hearing officer will issue a written ruling within five to ten days.

h. Parents are allowed, to have the due process hearing open to the public, or closed to the public. A closed hearing means that only school representatives and witnesses may come to the hearing. Parents are allowed, to bring an advocate and people to assist them in the due process. An open hearing, means that anyone may come to the due process hearing. All of the hearings that I advocated at were closed, because I felt that it was very important to sequester witnesses. Some hearing officers will not sequester witnesses if the parent chooses to have an open hearing. Sequestration is critical, because it prevents school personnel from hearing each other testify.

i. Parents should also ask any questions that they have about due process. If an advocate or friend is helping you, make sure they tell the hearing officer that they are not and attorney. In my experience, most hearing officers, are understanding to advocates who are not attorneys.

11 After the first three-way phone conference, more phone conferences, may be scheduled, to discuss various issues. Write down any issues you would like to bring up during the phone conferences; and also take notes during phone conference. Ask for any clarification that you need as well as timelines; so that you don't miss them.

12. Parents should start preparing the witness lists, and the subpoenas. Usually, I sent the subpoenas for any witnesses from the school, directly to their attorney, and they made sure that they received them—but be sure and ask. Anything sent to the school's representative should be either hand delivered, or sent by certified mail return receipt, so that you have proof that they received it. Send the independent evaluator a subpoena also; by certified mail return receipt. Continue to go through the school records looking for any concrete evidence that can be used, during due process, to help your case. Use post it notes to mark anything that will help your case.

13. Take all of the documents that you are going to use, and place them in order of usage, and number them. I number the documents P1- to whatever number of documents that you have. Each document used in due process must be numbered. Write a document list that contains the numbers of the documents. A document list, must be given, to the school representative and the hearing officer. Keep several for yourself, to make preparation easier.

Then number each page starting with the first document first page and continue until each page is numbered. Make a list of what document starts on what page; to make it easier to find things in the hearing. This list, should also be given, to the school representative and the hearing officer, and several for yourself.

Make holes in any documents that need them; and put them in # order in a large binder. You may need more than one binder.

Remember you need a witness list, a document list, and a document binder for yourself, the school district and also for the hearing officer. The school's representative, must receive all written information, that will be used at the due process hearing, **at least five business days before the hearing.** I made sure they got their copies around seven to eight days before the hearing. The cost of copying the records is the major expense for a due process hearing. Check around and see of you can save any money on this, by making the copies yourself. Usually the hearing officer gets their information at the hearing, but be sure and ask him or her when they want them. Check the lists and the binders several times before giving them to the school representative and the hearing officer. One time, I left a Post-It note on a document, and the school's attorney became enraged, because she thought the hearing officer had seen it. He actually laughed about it, but I bet he wondered what was on that Post-It note! Have another person check the binders also, just to make sure that all notes have been taken off.

14. Parents should study the documents as much as they can, so that if an issue is brought up during the due process hearing, they know which document to use to counteract the testimony. The attorney that I went up against was surprised that I knew what each document contained, and where to find what I needed, at a moments notice. Knowing what is in the documents, is extremely important, and could take hundreds of hours, but it is worth it.

15. During the pre-hearing conference, try to schedule the due process hearing, at least thirty to sixty days in the future; to allow for enough time for preparation. Also, if a witness is testifying by telephone, make sure that a conference telephone is available.

16. Prepare questions for witnesses; this could take many hours. I type them on my computer, and actually print them the night before. This allows me to change the questions, as I need to, before I actually print them. Put the questions in a binder for the due process hearing, and don't forget to add paper to the end for questions that you want to add during the due process. Change the questions during the hearing as

necessary. **The questions for school employees should be yes or no questions only**. If a parent asks an open-ended question, they will not know what the witness is going to say. Parents should ask school personnel, a lot of questions about documents that help their case. For Example: In the due process hearing that I advocated at, where the school teacher stated that the restrictive program, was not appropriate for the young man. I did not ask her if she made the statement: instead I handed her the letter (documenting the conversation), and had her read it, out loud, into the record. I asked her if the mother had handed her a copy of this letter, and she said yes. (The school district had implied, in their case, that the school teacher did not agree with the content of the conversation). I asked the school teacher, while she was on the stand, if she had written a letter to the mother stating that this was not the way she remembered the conversation; she said no. Since the teacher did not write a letter stating that she remembered the conversation differently, it implied that the mother's version of the conversation was truthful. In my opinion, the hearing officer, believed the mothers testimony.

17. Make sure that all of the issues that you filed for are addressed with the questions. Also, write questions to rebut what you think the schools case is. During the due process hearing, make sure that you use all of the documents that were included in your binder, or the schools representative may ask the hearing officer to exclude them. Use documents that help your case, to ask questions for each witness, and as many times as you can. This will strengthen your case.

18. Type up, a tentative opening and closing statement. I say "tentative" because your statement may change during the hearing. Make your opening and closing simple, and not too long; keep it to one or two pages. Be sure and add laws from IDEA 2004 and case law that supports your case.

19. Make arrangements, with the independent evaluator to testify at the hearing. If the evaluator absolutely cannot come to the hearing in person, or wants to charge too much to do so, have the evaluator testify by telephone. Make certain this is set up

with the school and hearing officer, and that a conference telephone is available. I have used this as a last resort; but I prefer if the evaluator testifies in person.

20. Enlarge your graphs and any other evidence that you will be using at due process hearing. Graphs can be enlarged, at any office supply store.

21. If the school district representative notifies you that they would like to settle the case, tell them that you will consider it, but only if the settlement is in writing, and is done by a consent decree. While IDEA 2004 has added language about written settlement agreements; these must be enforced in state or federal court. A consent decree, is done by the hearing officer reading the settlement into the record, with a court reporter taking it down. A consent decree, is treated like a due process hearing officers ruling, and is enforceable by your state department of education. I was thankful that another advocate told me about this, and I used it when I settled one of the cases that I advocated at. Some states may not allow consent decrees; check with your state board of education.

22 At least five business days before the hearing any documents etc. to be used, must be given to the other party. If you mail them, send them certified mail return receipt requested. Also, make sure they are in the other parties, hands at least five school days before the hearing. Any documents, not given to the other party five days ahead of time, cannot be used.

Due Process Hearing

1. Go in the room and set all of your evidence up. Put the documents and lists in front of you, within easy reach. Have one of your friends prepared to take a lot of notes, and watch the hearing officer. This is important, because the parent will be too busy working on the case, to do these things. I do take a lot of notes though, but sometimes I would miss something, and the other person could fill me in. Any last minute business, will be discussed, followed by opening arguments.

2. If the witnesses are sequestered, make sure they are not in the room listening to other school personnel testify. If you are allowed to go first; call your first witness.

Ask them their name, for the record, and ask them to spell it. Then begin asking questions. After the school representative asks questions, the parent will be able to ask the witness more questions; this is called rebuttal. Remember any documents that you use must be testified to, by a witness; or the schools representative may ask that the document be excluded. Write post it notes to communicate with the other people helping you. Take breaks when necessary. Try really hard, to keep your composure no matter what happens. In my second due process I was asking questions of the school districts superintendent. She did not want to answer any of my questions. She kept saying "Why do you need to know that". The hearing officer lost his patience quickly and told her to answer the questions. I actually got a kick out of it; a little lightness in a brutal process. The parent should testify last. If you are conducting your own due process hearing, have some one else ask you the questions.

Remember to stay away from the BEST word. If the school representative asks you any question with the "B" word in it; red flags should go up. Say, "No, I am here today trying to get an appropriate education for my child."

3. While the schools witnesses are testifying, take notes, change questions, write new questions, and gather documents for rebuttal.

4. You can make objections (which the school's representative will probably also be doing). Most of the objections that I heard were related to relevance, but I think the objections were done to rattle me--which they did not.

5. The hearing may take a couple of days. This will give you overnight to regroup, and get ready for the next day.

6. Re-write your closing argument. In one case, the attorney asked that she be allowed to give her closing argument in writing. I did not object, but stated that I still wanted to give my closing argument verbally, which the hearing officer allowed me to do. A few days after the hearing, the attorney sent me a copy of her written closing argument; which she had already sent to the hearing officer.

7. The hearing officer must make a ruling within ten days. In one of the hearings that I advocated at; the school and I had to notify the Illinois State Board of Education because the hearing officer hadn't sent the ruling; and it had been over a month.

8. After the due process ruling, either side can appeal to state or federal court if they lose the due process hearing, within ninety days. This was changed from one hundred and twenty days to ninety days in IDEA 2004.

Parents can conduct, their own child's due process hearing. It takes a lot of preparation but it is worth it, for your child to receive the services they need. If school personnel are not truthful while they are testifying, try and show this with your documents and the parents testimony.

Due process is not all serious. During one particular grueling hearing, the person who was helping me, and I, sent funny post it notes back and forth to each other. At the end of the hearing, we went to a coffee shop and read them. We laughed, and laughed, and couldn't, figure half of them out. Keep the due process simple, focus on the due process issues, and do the best you can, for your child.

Appendix B: Quick Guide to Acronyms Used in This Book

ADD: Attention Deficit Disorder

ADHD: Attention Deficit Hyperactivity Disorder

COPAA: The Council of Parent Attorneys and Advocates

EIS: Early Intervention System

FAPE: Free Appropriate Public Education

IAES: Interim Alternative Educational Setting

IDEA: The Individuals with Disabilities Education Act

IDEA 2004: The Individuals with Disabilities Education Act 2004

IEE: Independent Education Evaluation

IEP: Individual Education Plan

LEA: Local Educational Agency (local school district)

LRE: Least Restrictive Environment

NICHCY: National Information Center for Children and Youth With Disabilities

NCLB: No Child Left Behind Act

OSEP: The Office of Special Education Programs

OSERS: The Office of Special Education and Rehabilitative Services

PTIC: The Parent Training and Information Centers

SEA: State Educational Agency (state board of education)

Appendix C: Easy-to-Understand Definitions

1. ADHD: Attention Deficit Hyperactivity Disorder. There is also a diagnosis that is called ADD. ADD is Attention Deficit Disorder, which differs from ADHD because there is no hyperactivity.

2. ADHD rating scale: A written scale that helps determine if a child has ADHD. The scale is filled out by parents, the teacher, or both. The most common rating scale for ADHD is the Connors Rating Scale.

3. Advocate: A person who helps other people, receive their rights. In the context of this book, an advocate, is someone who helps parents navigate their way through the special education system, so that their child can receive an appropriate education.

4. Advocacy: The act of working with parents to help ensure that their child receive an appropriate education

5 .Autism: A neurological disorder that impairs behavior, communication and social relationships. The prevalence of Autism has increased at an alarming rate in the last several years.

6. Autism rating scale: A written scale that helps determine if a child has autism. There are many autism rating scales, but in my opinion, the best one for children is the Childhood Autism Rating Scale (CARS).

7. Consent Forms: A form that parents must sign to give permission for school districts to perform initial evaluations, and reevaluations. If a child, is found eligible for special education services, then the parent must also sign a consent form for initial special education services. A consent form can also be completed if a parent or the school district, wants the school to share information with another entity.

8. Continuum of placement options: Every school district is required under IDEA 2004, to offer a continuum of placement options: from regular classrooms, to special classes to specials schools. If a school does not offer a needed placement, they must make arrangements, with another school district to accommodate the child, or pay for a private placement.

9. Core Academic Subjects: Defined in the NCLB act as English, Reading, Language Arts, Math, Science, Foreign Languages, Civics, Government, Economics, History, and Geography.

10. Department of Education ,US: The agency run by the federal government that is responsible for education in the United States. DOE monitors school districts compliance with all educational laws, is involved with research about what educational programs work, it enforces NCLB, and many other functions. Other than the courts, the US Department of Education is the final federal authority on education in the USA. The Office of Special Education Programs (OSEP) is the part of the department of education that deals with special education. OSEP is part of the Office of Special Education and Rehabilitation Services (OSERS).

11. District-an-State-Wide Testing: Standardized tests given by the district, or required by the state, to determine the academic levels of students. The testing also lets schools and parents know if the child is at grade and age equivalent levels. NCLB requires that all children take district-and-state- wide assessments, unless the IEP team agrees otherwise.

12. Due process hearing: A formal hearing initiated by parents or school districts, to resolve special education disputes. Due process is heard in front of a hearing officer, not a judge.

13. Early Intervention System: This system provides services to infants and children with disabilities, from birth to age three. The early intervention system, is covered under Part C, of IDEA 2004.

14. FAPE: Free Appropriate Public Education. This is defined as special education services that "confer educational benefit." FAPE is difficult for parents and school districts to agree on, and disputes often end up in due process.

15. Functional Behavioral Assessment: This is a process that tries to determine, what a child is gaining from a certain behavior. The assessment includes information about the behavior, what was happening before the behavior, consequences of the

behavior, and the functional intent. The assessment is usually done by the child's teacher (if they are trained), or the IEP team.

16. IDEA: The Individuals with Disabilities Education Act. This was changed in 2004 to the Individuals with Disabilities Education Improvement Act of 2004. Special education services for children from three years of age through age 21, are covered under Part B of IDEA 2004.

17.IEP: The Individual Education Plan. Any child with a disability, who is eligible for special education services, must have an IEP developed by the IEP team. The most important part, is that they plan must be **individualized.**

18. IEP team: The IEP team consists of the parents, the regular education teacher (if the child is receiving services in regular education), the special education teacher, the principal, an assistant or aide that works with your child, any related service persons, if appropriate. The IEP team basically, includes all people who work with your child during school. If your child is in high school, and has many teachers they should all be a part of the IEP team; and attend the IEP meeting.

19. Interim Alternative Educational Setting: This refers to an educational placement outside of the regular school building, or district. IDEA 2004 allows school personnel to place a child in an IAES, for forty five days, if the child brought a gun, or drugs to school. IDEA 2004 also allows placement in an IAES if a child has caused serious bodily injury to another person during the school day. If school personnel want to keep a student in the IAES for more than 45 days, they must prove to a hearing officer that it is necessary for the safety of the student or other students. Parents must be careful that any IAES that school personnel want to place their child in continues to provide the educational services that are in the child's IEP.

20. Learning Disabilities: (also known as specific learning disabilities): A disorder in one or more of the psychological areas, that affects a child's ability to understand or use language. The language can be spoken or written and may show itself in a child having trouble listening, thinking, speaking, reading, spelling, math. This also includes perception disabilities, and dyslexia.

21. Least Restrictive Environment: Children with disabilities have the right to be educated with children without disabilities. Placement decisions should begin with the regular classroom, and only become more restrictive, if the child's disability warrants it.

22 Mental retardation: Significantly below average general intellectual functioning, existing with deficits in adaptive behavior, and occurring during the child's developmental period. This also negatively affects the child's educational performance.

23. Multi sensory Reading Program: A reading program that utilizes these five principles

a. Simultaneous multi sensory (affects all senses at the same time)

b. Systematic and cumulative

c. Direct interaction

d. Diagnostic teaching, and

e. Synthetic and analytic Instruction #3 This definition was taken from the Orton-Gillingham Website, and was used with permission. **www.ortongillingham.com.**

24. Office of Special Education Programs (OSEP), which is part of OSERs Both are part of the U.S. Department of Education.

25. Parent Training and Information Centers (PTIC's). Each state must have at least one. The centers provide training and information about special education to help parents with their child's education.

26. Related Services: Means services that are required to help a child with disabilities to benefit from their education. The list of related services is endless, whatever the child needs to benefit from their education. For example: transportation, therapy (physical, occupational, or speech therapy or others), school health services, recreation, audiology services etc. If a child needs therapy under related services, parents should make sure that the child receives direct instruction, and not consultation. Related services could also include tutoring, if a child needs it.

27. Scientifically based research: A term that is used, to describe curriculum, that has been developed based on research and analysis, and that these approaches are proven to teach children.

28. School psychologist: A credentialed professional who works for a school district; who performs educational and psychological testing on children to determine if they have a disability, and do reevaluations of children already identified as having a disability. When the testing is complete, the school psychologist writes a report, interpreting the test results. This is the area, where I often disagree with school psychologists. A lot of them interpret the test results in the schools favor, and parents often do not understand this. If the tests are low they say that the child doesn't test well, rather than stating the truth; which is that the child's academics are at a low level, and they require educational remediation. Remediation means that educational services, are given to the child with disabilities, to help them reach age and grade appropriate scores in all academic areas.

29. Self-Contained placement: A special education program, outside of the regular classroom, that provides special education services. For a child to be considered to be in a self-contained placement they must be in the class at least fifty percent of the school day.

30. Special Education: Is defined as "Specially designed instruction, at no cost to the parents, to meet the unique needs of a child with a disability. Special education is a program that is individually designed for your child, taking into account their disability and educational needs. Special education is also defined, as a service, not a placement. If it is appropriate, a child can be educated in a regular classroom and receive special education services; or be in a self-contained class.

31. Special Education Cooperative: School districts sometimes come together to provide special education services "cooperatively" (or together). Where I live, the special education cooperative has thirteen school districts that work together to provide services. Some programs may be located in the cooperative, or located in one of the school districts. The cooperative provides staff and supervises special

educators in the districts that belong to the cooperative. Most disabilities are considered "low incidence" (they don't occur very often). The cooperative agreement allows school districts to provide services for these "low incidence" disabilities. In Michigan, the classes are located in the Intermediate (county), school district.

32. Special Education Coordinator or Director. A person that works for a school district, who supervises all special education personnel; and special education programs. The coordinator also conducts IEP meetings, and is part of the IEP team.

33. State Board of Education: The state agency, responsible for monitoring the compliance of all education laws. Each state board of education has a special education department to monitor schools compliance with IDEA 2004. State boards of educations also take individual and systemic complaints from parents, and make decisions about which side is right and which side is wrong.

State board of educations have other jobs including being in charge of due process training and appointing of due process hearing officers.

34. State complaints: A formal complaint, by a parent, to the state board of education, that states that their school district violated IDEA 2004.

35. Transition Services: Services that are for a young person who is sixteen years if age (or younger if the IEP team think that it is necessary) to help them transition to adult life. These services should be based on each child's needs, preferences, and interests. Transition services should be outcome oriented, and help the young person prepare for college, vocational training, integrated employment, and independent living.

36. Woodcock Reading Mastery Test: A standardized Reading test that can be given by a teacher or a school psychologist. The reason I like to ask for this test is because it not only gives a reading score (grade and age equivalent), but also gives a vocabulary and a decoding score. I learned in my advocacy that one reason that children with disabilities do not increase their reading level, is because of poor vocabulary skills or difficulty with decoding.

Appendix D: Resources

1. Attainment Company: Books and other resources at **www.atainmentcompany.com**. Phone 1-800-651-0954.

2. Autism Resource Network Website **www.autismbooks.com.** Phone 1-952-988-0099.

3. Bazelon Center for Mental Health Law can be reached at their Website **www.bazelon.org.** 1101 15th St NW Suite 1212 Washington Dc. 20005 Phone 1-202-467-5730.

4. Beach Center on Family and Disabilities. **www.beachcenter.org.** University of Kansas 3136 Haworth Hall 1200 Sunny side Ave Lawrence Ks.66045. This organization provides information on behavioral difficulties and strategies to deal with them.

5. Centers for Independent Living in the USA available at the Website **www.virtualcil.net/cils.**

6. Center on Positive Behavioral Interventions and Support **www.pbis.org.** 1761 Alder St. 1235 College of Education Eugene OR. 97403 1-541-346-2505.

7. CHADD which stands for children and adults with attention deficit disorders is available at the Website **www.chadd.org.**
Children's Disabilities Information can be reached at the Website **www.childrensdisabilities.info.com.** This website contains a lot of information about different disabilities, that will be helpful to parents.

8. Circle of Inclusion University of Kansas Department of Special Education 521JR Pearson, Lawrence Ks. 66045 1-785-864-0685 website **www.circleofinclusion.org.** There is a lot of different information on this site for parents. I found some wonderful behavioral forms that parents can download and use.

9. Closing the Gap is an organization that gives information on computer technology in special education and rehabilitation. **www.closingthegap.com.** 1-507-248-3294.

10. COPPA stands for the Council of Parent Attorneys and Advocates. Yearly Membership is reasonable, and gives parents a lot of resources. Their Website is **www.copaa.com.**

11. Council for Exceptional Children can be reached at their Website **www.cec.sped.org.**

12. Don Johnston books and other materials. Their Website is **www.donjohnston.com**. Phone 1-800-999-4660.

13. Enabling Devices can be reached at their Website **www.enablingdevices.com.** Phone 1-800-832-8697.

14. Exceptional Parent magazine can be found at their Website **www.eparent.com.** Phone 1-877-372-7368.

15. Federation for Families for Children's Mental Health's Website is **www.ffcmh.org.**

16. Illinois Assistive Technology Program's Website is **www.iltech.org.**

17. Katy Beckett Waiver information. The Katy Becket waiver allows children with life long medical needs, to receive Medicaid, despite their parents income. They can be reached at the Website **www.specialfriends.org.**

18. Lovaas Institute on ABA/Lovaas programs, can be reached at the Website **www.lovaas.com.**

19. National Council for Disabilities 1331 First St. N.W. Suite 850 Washington D.C. Their Website is **www.ncd.gov.**

20. National Center for Learning Disabilities Inc. Their Website is **www.LD.org.** They have a wonderful Learning Disabilities Checklist that parents can use as a resource.

21. National Down Syndrome Society's Website is **www.ndss.org.**

22. National Information Center for Children and Youth with Disabilities (NICHCY) P.O. Box 1492 Washington Dc. 20013 1-800-695-0285 **www.nichcy.org.** I love this website. All kinds of wonderful information available.

For behavior the NICHCY Website is

http://www.nichcy.org/resources/behavassess.asp.

23. No Child Left Behind Parent Guide can be ordered at the Website

www.nclb.gov/next/.

24. Orton Gillingham methodolology can be reached at their Website

www.ortongillingham.com. The Institute for Multi SensoryEducation 1000 S. Old

Woodward Suite 105 Birmingham Michigan 48009 Telephone1-800-646-9788

25. PACERS Center 8161 Normandale Blvd. Minneapolis MN. 55437 1-952-838-

9000. Their Website is **www.pacer.org.**

26. ProEd is available at the website **www.proedinc.com.** They publish a lot of tests

that parents can use as a resource.8700 Shoal Creek Blvd. Autstin Tx. 78757A book

on ABA programs

can be purchased at this Website. Entitled *Behavioral Intervention For Young*

Children With Autism edited by Catherine Maurice and Co edited by Gina Green and

Stephen C. Luce

27. Reed Martin Esq. can be reached at his Website **www.reedmartin.com.** Read

Naturally's Website is **www.readnaturally.com.** Phone 1-651-452-4085.

28. TASH can be reached at their Website **www.tash.org.** 1025 Vermont Ave. Floor

seven Washington Dc. 20005. I found a booklet that a lot of parents may need on

restraints, and other types of behavioral interventions. *In the Name of Treatment: A*

parents Guide to protecting your child from the use of restraint, aversive

interventions and seclusion. It can be downloaded from their website or ordered.

29. The Arc of the US can be reached at their Website

www.thearc.org.

30. The Florida Center for Reading Research can be reached at their Web site

www.fcrr.org.

31. US Department of Educations Website is **www.ed.gov.** Policy letters can be

found by typing in he box (Special Education policy letters). Model form can also be down loaded from **http://idea.ed.gov.** Model forms are written in the areas of IEP's, prior written notice (PWN), and procedural safeguards.

32. Wrightslaw which is run by Pam and Peter Wright is found at their Website **www.wrightslaw.com.**

Bibliography

1. Steedman Wayne Esq. "10 Tips: How to Use IDEA 2004 to Improve your Child's Special Education". Article found on Wrightslaw **www.wrightslaw.com.** Used with permission from Wayne Steedman Esq.

2. "Functional Behavioral Assesment and Positive Interventions: What Parents Need to Know." PACER Center can be reached at **www.pacer.org;** or 8161 Normandale Blvd. Minneapolis MN, 1-952-838-9000. Reprintedwith permission from PACER Center. All rights reserved.

3. Institute for Multi Sensory Education can be reached at the Website **www.ortongillingham.com.** Used for the definition of Multi Sensory Curriculum. 1000 S. Old Woodward, Suite 105 Birmingham, Mi. 48009. Used with permission.

Order Form

Name: _____

Address: _____

City: _____ State:_____

Zip: _____ Telephone #:_____

Email address: _____

Cost of book: $19.95

Sales Tax: Please add 6.25% for products shipped to Illinois addresses.

Shipping: $5.00 for the first book and $2.50 for each additional book.

Payments by check only

Or this book can be purchased at the website **www.disabilitydeception.com.**

Or at JoAnn Collins Publishing

PO Box 89

Bradley Il. 60915

This is an Example of a school district letter to a parent.

Cindy Landry
645 Thornton Rd.
Mayfield Il. 60988

May 1, 20—

Dear Miss Landry:

    As you are aware, we have been having difficulty with your son Sam's behavior. This letter is to inform you, that the IEP team has decided to change Sam's placement to the Behavioral Institute. The Behavioral Institute is located 90 minutes away, in the city of Levenworth Il. Your son Sam kicked his teacher on Friday, and that is the reason, why his placement, is being changed. The bus driver will call you, within the next few days, to set up his bus schedule. IDEA 2004, states that school districts, have the right to change children with disibilitie's placement, because of their behavior.

Sincerely,

Mary Smith

Nelson School District

1589 Staton Dr.

This is an example of a letter from a parent, written in response to the above letter.

Mary Smith
Nelson School District
1589 Staton Dr.
Mayfield Il. 60988

May 3, 20—

Dear Mrs. Smith:

As you are aware, my son Sam, has received special education services under the identifying characteristics of Other Health Impaired (for his ADHD), and Learning Disabilities since he was five years old. Sam is now seven years old, and is in second grade. Sam has had difficulty with his behavior since he began school two years ago. His last IEP dated September 20—states that Sam's behavior interferes with his education. I asked at that meeting (at the beginning of this school year), that a functional behavioral assessment be performed, by a trained staff member, to determine why Sam, continues to have behavioral difficulties. You stated at that time, that you did not believe that he needed it. A positive behavioral plan, was written, and attached to his IEP.

According to IDEA 2004, the parent is to be an equal member of the IEP team. I was not included in the meeting, where a decision was made, to change my son's placement. Therefore, I believe that the decision to change my son's placement was not done in a legal manner. If the school district continues to push for a change in my son's placement, I may have to file for a due process hearing.

I have had several discussions with Sam's teacher, throughout the school year. I have come to the conclusion, that Sam's positive behavioral plan, is not being following. One example, is that Sam's IEP states that I will get a daily behavioral sheet, which I have not received for the entire year; even though I have reminded her several times. Sam's teacher states that she does not have the time to fill one out. Another concern about Sam's behavior is that he is being ridiculed in the classroom, which only makes the situation worse.

In IDEA 2004 300.530 under (e)(1) states "within ten school days of any decision to change the placement of a child with a disability because of a violation of a code of student conduct, the local educational agency and member of the IEP team must review all relevant information in the student's file, including the child's IEP, to determine: a. If the conduct was caused by the child's disability, and b. If the conduct in question was the direct result of the LEA's failure to implement the IEP."

Within ten school days of May first, a manifestation determination review must be held for my son Sam, according to IDEA 2004. I believe that Sam's behavior is not only a part of his disability, but it is also caused, by the non-compliance with his IEP. I expect a written notice to come within a few days. IDEA 2004 requires a ten day written notice for meetings. I will waive the ten day written notice, so that the manifestation determination review can be done by May 11, 20—. At that time, we can discuss the need for a functional behavioral analysis, and an update to his positive behavior plan.

I understand that Sam, kicked his teacher when she lunged at him, while he was upset. I have spoken to her, on the telephone, Friday afternoon, and she states that she was not injured. IDEA 2004, allows for a change of placement to a IAES for forty five school days for carrying a weapon, drugs, or causing serious bodily injury on school grounds. Sam's teacher was not injured, he did not have a weapon, and there were no drugs involved. Therefore, I do not believe that IDEA 2004, would allow you to place Sam in an IAES, for forty five school days.

Also, state and federal rules only allow children to stay on a bus sixty minutes each way. Ninety minutes each way is too long, and Sam would not tolerate this.

I am not agreeing, at this time, to change Sam's placement. Sam will continue to attend school, until after the manifestation determination meeting. I expect to hear from you, within a few days, to set up the mandatory manifestation determination review.

Cindy Landry
645 Thornton Rd.
Mayfield Il. 60988